Christmas with the Presidents

Christmas with the Presidents

*Holiday Lessons for
Today's Kids from America's Leaders*

Mike Henry

ROWMAN & LITTLEFIELD
Lanham • Boulder • New York • London

Published by Rowman & Littlefield
A wholly owned subsidiary of The Rowman & Littlefield Publishing Group, Inc.
4501 Forbes Boulevard, Suite 200, Lanham, Maryland 20706
www.rowman.com

Unit A, Whitacre Mews, 26-34 Stannary Street, London SE11 4AB

Copyright © 2018 by Mike Henry

All rights reserved. No part of this book may be reproduced in any form or by any electronic or mechanical means, including information storage and retrieval systems, without written permission from the publisher, except by a reviewer who may quote passages in a review.

British Library Cataloguing in Publication Information Available

Library of Congress Cataloging-in-Publication Data

Names: Henry, Mike, 1952– author.
Title: Christmas with the presidents / holiday lessons for today's kids from America's leaders / Mike Henry.
Description: Lanham : Rowman & Littlefield, 2017. | Includes bibliographical references.
Identifiers: LCCN 2017043042 (print) | LCCN 2017044477 (ebook) | ISBN 9781475837841 (Electronic) | ISBN 9781475837827 (cloth : alk. paper) | ISBN 9781475837834 (pbk. : alk. paper)
Subjects: LCSH: Presidents—United States—Biography—Miscellanea—Juvenile literature. | Christmas—United States--History.
Classification: LCC E176.1 (ebook) | LCC E176.1 .H453 2017 (print) | DDC 973.09/9—dc23
LC record available at https://lccn.loc.gov/2017043042

∞™ The paper used in this publication meets the minimum requirements of American National Standard for Information Sciences—Permanence of Paper for Printed Library Materials, ANSI/NISO Z39.48-1992.

Printed in the United States of America

Contents

Preface: Christmas Greetings		ix
1	GEORGE WASHINGTON Danger on the Delaware	1
2	JOHN ADAMS The First White House Christmas	3
3	THOMAS JEFFERSON Grandpa Played the Fiddle	7
4	JAMES MADISON Dinner with Dolley	9
5	JAMES MONROE A Christmas Never Forgotten	13
6	JOHN QUINCY ADAMS The President and the Christmas Eve Flower	15
7	ANDREW JACKSON A Christmas for the Orphans	17
8	MARTIN VAN BUREN A Dutch Christmas	21
9	JOHN TYLER Waiting for Julia	25
10	JAMES K. POLK The Christmas Wedding	27
11	ZACHARY TAYLOR Christmas in Many Places	31
12	MILLARD FILLMORE Together Again	33
13	FRANKLIN PIERCE The First Christmas Tree	37
14	JAMES BUCHANAN A Divided Christmas	39
15	ABRAHAM LINCOLN The Soldiers and Christmas	41

16	ANDREW JOHNSON	A Christmas Pardon	45
17	ULYSSES S. GRANT	An Official Holiday	47
18	RUTHERFORD B. HAYES	Sharing Christmas Cheer	51
19	CHESTER ARTHUR	Nell's Helping Hands	53
20	GROVER CLEVELAND	Holiday Changes	57
21	BENJAMIN HARRISON	The President with the White Beard	61
22	WILLIAM MCKINLEY	Tough Times at Christmas	63
23	THEODORE ROOSEVELT	Bah-Humbug!	67
24	WILLIAM HOWARD TAFT	Christmas Wishes Do Come True	71
25	WOODROW WILSON	Christmas Connections	75
26	WARREN HARDING	Helping Others at Christmas	79
27	CALVIN COOLIDGE	Let's Light the Tree!	83
28	HERBERT HOOVER	The White House Is on Fire.... Again!	87
29	FRANKLIN D. ROOSEVELT	The 12 Years of Christmas	91
30	HARRY S. TRUMAN	Christmas in Independence	95
31	DWIGHT D. EISENHOWER	The Painting President	99
32	JOHN F. KENNEDY	The Christmas Theme	103
33	LYNDON B. JOHNSON	A Texas-Sized Christmas	107
34	RICHARD NIXON	New Traditions	111
35	GERALD FORD	Christmas on the Slopes	115
36	JIMMY CARTER	A Small Town Christmas	119
37	RONALD REAGAN	The Meaning of Christmas	123
38	GEORGE H.W. BUSH	A Cherry Picker for Christmas	127
39	BILL CLINTON	Peace on Earth	131
40	GEORGE W. BUSH	Remembrance and Goodwill	135
41	BARACK OBAMA	The Christmas Letter	139
42	DONALD J. TRUMP	The Gift of Giving	141
43	That Special Time of the Year: White House Christmas Themes		145
44	Valley Forge and the Christmas of 1777		155

Epilogue (William Henry Harrison and James Garfield)	161
Answer Key for Today's Questions	165
References	169
About the Author	177

Preface
Christmas Greetings

Since 1789, forty-five different men have served as president of the United States. Some were tall, like Abraham Lincoln, but others were short, like James Madison. Some of them came from wealthy families like John F. Kennedy while there were those who knew about going through hard times such as Ulysses S. Grant.

But they all had one thing in common; they celebrated Christmas in their own unique way. Each year, we see a number of families enjoy the holiday in their special manner—some with big festivals, others with small parties. The wonderful part is that there are no rules when it comes to observing Christmas.

This book tells the stories of how our presidents observed the holiday season. Like the rest of us, each of them had their own way to celebrate. There will be a few surprises, like the Roosevelt's Christmas of 1902, that will make you chuckle while a tragic event that had taken place meant that nothing could bring happiness to the Coolidge family in 1924.

Everyone realizes that the president has a great deal of power, however like all citizens, they must be careful because there is someone out there who is checking to see if, just like the rest of us, they've been naughty or nice.

Enjoy the holiday season and Merry Christmas!

George Washington and his troops crossing the Delaware River on Christmas night 1776 (National Archives image/Emanuel Leutze, artist).

CHAPTER 1

George Washington
The 1st President
Danger on the Delaware

George Washington served two terms as president of the United States. That means that he celebrated eight years of winter holidays as the nation's leader. However, one of his most important contributions to America's freedom took place during one Christmas before he was president.

It was in 1776 when he was the commanding general for the U.S. Continental Army during the Revolutionary War. Things had not been going well for the American soldiers in their fight for independence from the British. In fact, it was so bad that many of them were simply quitting the army and returning to their homes.

General Washington came up with a plan that he hoped would win an important battle and inspire the volunteers to remain with the military. But it wasn't going to be easy.

On Christmas night 1776, the general, along with more than 2,000 men were in Pennsylvania. At about 11:00 pm, they began to make their move by loading into boats in order to cross the Delaware River. It was difficult for the soldiers to steer the small crafts because of the cold and windy weather along with the ice that had formed on top of the water. They were also unable to use their lanterns for fear of being spotted by the enemy.

Crossing the river placed the soldiers in New Jersey. After leaving their boats, the troops began a nine-mile march through the snow to the town of Trenton. It was there that more than 1,000 German soldiers known as Hessians (pronounced Hesh-ans), who were fighting on the side of the British, were in camp.

After crossing the Delaware River and then marching for miles through the snow, General Washington's army attacked the Hessians in Trenton at 8:00 am, the morning after Christmas. Many of the German soldiers were still asleep after celebrating the night before as the Americans moved in. Following a short battle, the Hessians surrendered.

General Washington's plan was a huge Christmas present because the victory at Trenton helped inspire many American soldiers to stay in the army and five years later, the British were finally defeated. That meant all U.S. citizens, including those who are living today and into the future, would have freedom.

TODAY'S QUESTIONS

1. Who was the commanding general of the American Army?
2. What was the name of the river that was crossed by the American Army?
3. After the soldiers crossed the river, what state had they entered? New Jersey or New York?

IT'S A FACT . . .

In 1789, George Washington celebrated the first Christmas of a U.S. president. The White House had yet to be built so the First Couple enjoyed the holiday at the presidential residence in New York City.

President Washington was busy holding a meeting with Secretary of War Henry Knox and attending services at St. Paul's Church. Later, he and Mrs. Washington greeted visitors who dropped by to offer holiday greetings. For her gift, the First Lady received a set of pearl earrings from the Father of Our Country.

Yes, it's true!

Chapter 2

John Adams
The 2nd President
The First White House Christmas

Have you ever celebrated Christmas after moving to a new place? It's always an exciting experience. For the country's second president, John Adams, the Christmas of 1800 was a special event.

It was the first to be celebrated at the White House. John and First Lady Abigail Adams had only been in their new surroundings for about a month, as workers were still busy trying to get things finished. The mansion was so large and since there was no electric or natural gas heating back then, the couple had to rely on constantly burning wood in its thirteen fireplaces in order to stay warm.

Mrs. Adams hung the laundry to dry inside the building's unfinished East Room because she didn't believe that it was proper to have the president's clothes dangling outside where the public could see them.

The Adamses also gave the first White House Christmas party in honor of their four-year-old granddaughter Susanna who lived with them as her father Charles had died just before the holiday. Back then, the White House was known as either the President's Palace, Presidential Mansion, or President's House. It wasn't officially named the White House until 1901.

At the party, which was held in the grand ballroom, there were musicians and lots of food including cake. Visitors had to be careful because some of the walls that had been recently painted had not yet dried. At one point, Susanna became angry with one of the other children who accidentally broke one of her new toys. But that wasn't the season's last celebration.

One week later, the Adamses gave the mansion's first New Year's Day party. It was open to the public with 135 visitors attending that gathering.

However, everything wasn't joyous for President Adams. A few weeks before Christmas, he had lost his reelection for another term as the country's leader which meant that these would be his last holidays for he and his family at the Presidential Palace. In March, he packed up his belongings and went home to Massachusetts where he celebrated future holidays at his family farm.

Even though they were there for just a short period of time, John Adams and his family did play an important part in the history of the White House. They were not just the first to live there but also the first to celebrate both Christmas and New Year's Day at the mansion.

Guests were arriving at the south entrance of the President's House in 1800 for its first Christmas party hosted by President John Adams (Illustration by Tom Freeman).

TODAY'S QUESTIONS

1. What was used to heat the White House during the time that the Adamses lived there?
2. Who was Susanna?
3. Why did President Adams celebrate only one Christmas at the White House?

It's a Fact . . .

It was so cold inside the White House on Christmas Day in 1800 that the First Family burned twenty cords of wood trying to keep warm. How much is that? It equals 2,560 cubic feet which is a lot of firewood.
 Yes, it's true!

At the White House Christmas party of 1805, President Jefferson and his violin were the stars of the evening (Illustration by Randy Jones).

Chapter 3

Thomas Jefferson
The 3rd President
Grandpa Played the Fiddle

In March 1801, John Adams became the first president to move out of the White House. Even though he had lived there for five months, many parts of the mansion remained unfinished. One of those areas was the massive East Room where the walls and ceiling had yet to be plastered. There were also several other areas in the building that needed work.

The next leader of the country was Thomas Jefferson who was supposed to move into the palace after Mr. Adams left. However, he didn't think that it was a good idea since the place still needed so much work. Also, the new president believed that the White House was simply too big for a normal sized family.

The truth was that Mr. Jefferson had a beautiful home at Monticello in Virginia which he had designed. He thought that he could run the country just as well from there, which was about 115 miles away, instead of Washington, D.C. But after some convincing, Mr. Jefferson and his family arrived at the White House which became their home for the next eight years.

President Jefferson believed in God and the freedom of religion but he didn't usually hold a large celebration for Christmas. He often spent those days doing one of the things that he enjoyed most—writing letters to friends or other family members. The president also liked spending time in the East Room that Abigail Adams had once used to hang and dry her laundry. However, Mr. Jefferson was often in there storing his valuable collection of dinosaur bones which he would usually spread across the floor.

But much of that changed in December 1805 when the nation's chief executive announced that he was going to give a huge Christmas party for six of his grandchildren which would be held at the White House. His wife had passed away before he became president so the first thing that he had to do was to find someone who would act as hostess of the gathering. His friend Dolley Madison took on the duty of helping prepare the mansion for the special day.

President Jefferson wanted to serve some good food to the guests so he personally walked to the market to pick out a Christmas goose for dinner. When the party got underway, more than 100 of his grandchildren's friends arrived at the palace to take part.

The highlight of the day was when the president picked up his violin and began playing. As he made music, the children danced and laughed with delight. Many had not known that President Jefferson had played the fiddle since he was a boy and, as a young man, had even written some music for the instrument.

When it was over, everyone had enjoyed a special Christmas celebration at the White House. But a few weeks later, President Jefferson received another gift.

On January 17, 1806, he welcomed the birth of another grandson to the First Family. James Madison Randolph made history as he became the first child to be born at the White House.

Today's Questions

1. What items did President Jefferson keep inside the East Room?
2. What musical instrument did President Jefferson play at the Christmas party?
3. What happened about three weeks after the Christmas party?

It's a Fact . . .

Do you like macaroni and cheese? If so, you might have Thomas Jefferson to thank for it. That's because in 1787, he drew up a plan for a machine that would turn dough into macaroni. It is believed that his daughter Mary began serving it with cheese during her time as hostess at the White House.

Yes, it's true!

Chapter 4

James Madison
The 4th President
Dinner with Dolley

Before he became president in 1809, James Madison was already well known to many people. He was one of America's Founding Fathers and wrote a number of items that are included in the United States Constitution. But he wasn't the only celebrity in the family as his wife Dolley was one of the most popular First Ladies in our country's history.

As you read in chapter 3, for many years, Dolley served as the official White House hostess for her friend Thomas Jefferson and helped put together many dinners and parties including those celebrating Christmas. When her husband became president, the holiday parties continued with dishes filled with seafood, stuffed goose, Virginia ham, and pound cake.

The Madisons welcomed a special guest to their first White House Christmas dinner party in 1811. Joining the president and First Lady was author Washington Irving who wrote *The Legend of Sleepy Hollow*.

Many times after everyone had eaten, the guests would sit down at a table and play "Loo." It was Dolley's favorite card game.

During the holidays, she enjoyed wearing a turban on her head with purple peacock feathers rising from it. During that period of history, people had not yet begun sending Christmas cards although the Madisons would write letters to their friends and relatives with good wishes for the holiday season. The First Lady became so popular that she was able to help get her husband reelected to a second term in 1812.

By 1814, the Madison's Christmas dinners had become the best known celebrations in Washington, D.C. However, they had to be changed during that year.

The United States was once again battling their old enemy Great Britain. This time it was during the War of 1812. In August 1814, the redcoats invaded the nation's capital and set many buildings, including the White House, on fire. Even though it wasn't completely burned down, there was still a great deal of damage. While the mansion was being repaired, the Madisons stayed in other places.

Their first move was to the Octagon House which was owned by the Tayloe family. It was one of the most beautiful homes in the city. It was there that the Madisons celebrated Christmas in 1814. That year, the United States won the war and received a special gift as they signed the peace treaty on Christmas Eve, 1814.

From October 1815 to March 1817, they lived at a different home in the Seven Buildings area of Washington, D.C. At their Christmas party in 1816, Dolley served ice cream and permitted her macaw parrot Uncle Willy to fly freely through the rooms. Having ice cream was difficult because there were no electric freezers back then.

After the White House was burned, the Madisons never lived there again. But that didn't keep them from happily celebrating Christmas with family and friends. Those good times continued for many years after they left Washington, D.C.

This is the White House Old Family Dining Room where the Madisons would enjoy meals and often entertain guests (whitehouse.gov photo).

TODAY'S QUESTIONS

1. Before her husband became president, Dolley Madison served as White House hostess for what other president?
2. What was Dolley's favorite card game?
3. Why were the Madisons forced to move from the White House?

IT'S A FACT . . .

Dolley Madison learned how to make ice cream from a former slave named Sallie Shadd. The First Lady heard about the dessert and traveled to Sallie's home in Delaware to try it. She enjoyed it so much that she had it served quite often at White House dinners and parties.

Yes, it's true!

This is a drawing from 1817 of the White House after it had been repaired following the War of 1812 (Library of Congress image).

Chapter 5

James Monroe
The 5th President
A Christmas Never Forgotten

Everyone has a special Christmas that they never forget. Even when they grow old and gray, the memory of that unique holiday remains with them. There was a president who had that type of Christmas, although it took place before he took office.

In chapter 1, you read about George Washington's troops crossing the Delaware River on Christmas night 1776. Among the more than 2,000 soldiers in the boats was an eighteen-year-old American officer named James Monroe.

Like General Washington, Lieutenant Monroe was from Virginia. When the troops reached Trenton, New Jersey, and the fighting began, a bullet grazed the left side of his chest and then struck his shoulder injuring an artery. Arteries are muscular tubes that deliver blood from the heart to the tissues of the body. But if one is damaged, it can be very dangerous.

Because of his wound, Lieutenant Monroe lost a great deal of blood. One of the doctors quickly stopped the bleeding by sticking his index finger into the gunshot hole and applying pressure to the artery. They believed that it would be too risky to remove the bullet so it remained in his shoulder. The lieutenant recovered about three months later.

Forty years afterward, James Monroe was elected president of the United States. He took office in March 1817. Later that year, he and his wife Elizabeth hosted their first Christmas celebration at the presidential mansion. It was there that their daughter Maria met Samuel Lawrence Gouverneur (pronounced Governor). Three years later, they were married in the first wedding ever held at the White House.

One week after the Christmas party, the Presidential Palace officially reopened on New Year's Day 1818. Workers had been busy trying to repair the damage that had been done by British soldiers during the War of 1812. One of the things that the mansion still needed was furniture. Many of the pieces that had been destroyed in the attack had not been replaced so the Monroes donated some of their own household furnishings. Today, there are nine of those pieces that remain in the White House and visitors can see them during a tour.

The other big news from the party that surprised many of the guests was that for the first time, the president's home had been painted white. Before the attack, it was a natural sandstone color but it was painted white to cover the burn marks left by the fires started by the enemy troops. It has remained that color since 1817 which is why today, it is called "The White House."

In 1824, the president received an important honor from the African country of Liberia during his last full year in office. The nation renamed its capital city Monrovia after the man from Virginia.

From being shot during the American Revolution to serving two terms as president of the United States, James Monroe lead a full and interesting life and still had time to celebrate Christmas.

Today's Questions

1. How did the doctor stop the bleeding in James Monroe's shoulder when he was wounded at the Battle of Trenton?
2. Where did President Monroe's daughter's wedding take place? Why did it make history?
3. Why was the presidential mansion painted white after the War of 1812?

It's a Fact . . .

On December 23, 1823, while James Monroe was president, a poem titled "A Visit from St. Nicholas" by Professor Clement Clarke Moore appeared in the *New York Sentinel* newspaper for the first time. It's still around today but you probably know this poem by its more common title, "The Night before Christmas."
Yes, it's true!

CHAPTER 6

John Quincy Adams
The 6th President
The President and the Christmas Eve Flower

Each year, there are special items that we see that only appear during the Christmas holidays. For example, houses that are decorated with wonderful lights. It doesn't matter what color they might be or how big the house is where they are displayed. These festive decorations help get everyone into the spirit of the season.

Can you name something that is usually only seen during Christmas time?

You might be thinking about a special plant that is often displayed through the holidays that is known as a poinsettia. It is a bloom with large red and green foliage that is often used as a Christmas decoration. Some other types of poinsettias have leaves that are white or pink. They can often be seen in stores and shopping malls during the holidays.

But what does the poinsettia plant have to do with the president? There is a twist to this story and here's the connection between the two.

In 1825, President John Quincy Adams appointed Congressman Joel R. Poinsett as the first U.S. ambassador to Mexico. One of his hobbies was botany which is the study of plants. While in the town of Taxco near Mexico City, Ambassador Poinsett was introduced to a plant that the local citizens called, "the Christmas Eve flower" and discovered that they grew in great numbers in southern Mexico. He found out that the ancient Aztec Indians once used the colorful blooms to make red dye and medicine.

The Aztecs were natives of Mexico who lived during the fourteenth, fifteenth, and sixteenth centuries. They worshipped the sun but in 1521, were overthrown by Spanish soldiers.

Ambassador Poinsett sent some of the plants to his home in Greenville, South Carolina, and gave them to many of his friends. Some began referring to them as "poinsettias" in honor of the ambassador and, after a few years, the name stuck.

So, the next time that you see a poinsettia at Christmastime, just remember that if President John Quincy Adams hadn't appointed Congressman Poinsett to become ambassador to Mexico, we might not have a traditional holiday plant!

The poinsettia plant is also known as the Christmas Eve flower (public domain image).

TODAY'S QUESTIONS

1. What are the colors of a poinsettia plant?
2. What did the Aztec Indians make from poinsettia plants?
3. In what country did Ambassador Poinsett first see the plants?

IT'S A FACT . . .

One year, President John Quincy Adams, refused to allow his sons John II and Charles to travel to Washington, D.C., for Christmas vacation. He didn't feel that his kids were doing well enough in their college classes. Instead, he sent them to their grandfather's house (former President John Adams) in Massachusetts to do more studying during the holidays.

Yes, it's true!

Chapter 7

Andrew Jackson
The 7th President
A Christmas for the Orphans

Most people who knew Andrew Jackson in the early 1800s believed that he was a tough guy. That was because he had fought and made it through the American Revolution and the War of 1812. In addition, as a young man, he had survived the deadly disease smallpox along with two gunshot wounds. The rugged man from Tennessee had also been involved in his share of fistfights.

But for all of his tenacity, there were two things that were close to President Jackson's heart—kids and Christmas. In 1828, he was elected to his first term in office but three days before Christmas, his beloved wife Rachel passed away. The couple had adopted three children and cared for several of their nephews and nieces. Without his wife, the new president suddenly became a single parent.

As sad as the holiday season was in 1828, it became a happy time a few years later in 1835 because President Jackson planned a special holiday celebration.

On Christmas Eve of that year, the president and his kids climbed into a carriage that took them to an orphanage in Washington, D.C. An orphanage is a home for children who have no parents to take care of them. During their journey, President Jackson told them the following story, "I once knew a little boy who not only never had a toy in his life, but after the death of his mother had neither home nor friends."

What the leader of the country didn't tell them was that the story was about his own life. His mother and brother died when he was young so he grew up as an orphan. That evening, the group in the carriage delivered Christmas gifts to the children who lived at the orphanage.

When they returned to the White House, the youngsters hung their Christmas stockings in the president's bedroom. Mr. Jackson, who was sixty-eight years old, joined them and, for the first time in his life, hung a stocking for himself. The next morning, everyone took down their long socks which had been filled with a silver quarter, candy, nuts, cake, fruit,

and a toy. The president received a pair of slippers and a pipe made from corncob.

A few days earlier, the Jackson family had sent out invitations to several children to attend a special Christmas Day celebration at the White House. These were some of the first Christmas cards that had ever been mailed from the mansion. That afternoon, guests arrived at the president's home where there were two hours of games, dancing, and singing.

That evening, the kids enjoyed a huge feast in the East Room that included wonderful dishes of food. The White House chef also made a sugar-frosted pine tree that was surrounded with toy animals made out of flavored ices. All of which could be eaten.

Later, the children participated in an indoor "snowball" fight with snowballs made from cotton.

For many years, Andrew Jackson didn't enjoy a happy Christmas holiday because he had been an orphan. But in 1835, he brought joy to children who were alone. That was the real gift that was given by the president.

Today's Questions

1. What did the Jacksons give to the children at the orphanage?
2. Where did the children hang their Christmas stockings?
3. Where did President Jackson hold the Christmas celebration for the children?

It's a Fact . . .

On Christmas Day 1830, when Andrew Jackson was president, the first regularly scheduled passenger train in the United States began serving customers. It traveled along a 136 mile route in South Carolina and, at the time, it was the longest railroad line in the world.

Yes, it's true!

A team of volunteers decorates the official White House Christmas Tree for 2009 in the Blue Room which was named by President Martin Van Buren (Official White House photo).

Chapter 8

Martin Van Buren
The 8th President
A Dutch Christmas

Martin Van Buren was the eighth president of the United States. He served from 1837 to 1841 but is not one of our best remembered leaders. However, he does have some interesting connections to the holiday season.

In 1631, Van Buren's great-great-great-grandfather Cornelis, who was from Holland, arrived with other Europeans at the settlement of New Netherland, that is today known as New York. The Van Burens eventually settled in the village of Kinderhook, which is about 130 miles from New York City, with many other Dutch immigrants.

Martin was born during the Christmas season in December 1782 in Kinderhook. He was the first president who was not born as a British subject or having British ancestors.

The Dutch are great believers in the most famous character of Christmas, Santa Claus. Although he is best known as the great deliverer of holiday gifts, his legend is actually based upon the story of Saint Nicholas, a Christian bishop who lived in the third century and became known as a protector of children and for helping those in need.

Throughout history, Saint Nicholas remained an important figure in Holland. The Dutch would celebrate him with a day of feast on December 6. It was a common practice for children to put out their shoes the night before. In the morning, they would discover them filled with the gifts that Saint Nicholas had left there for them. That tradition followed when a large number of Dutch immigrated to America.

Saint Nicholas became known as Sinterklaas and eventually became Santa Claus. The feast day also became part of the Christmas holiday.

Martin had grown up in a traditional Dutch family even though his parents were Americans. In 1807, he married his sweetheart Hannah Hoes (pronounced whose) who also came from a Dutch family in Kinderhook. In fact, the couple would speak Dutch when they were at home by themselves. Unfortunately, twelve years later, Hannah contracted the disease tuberculosis and died.

Martin never remarried, but his rising political career kept him busy. In 1829, he became governor of New York one week after Christmas. Two years later, he served as the U.S. Minister to England which allowed him to take part in an old-fashioned British Christmas celebration.

Traditionally, they would celebrate the twelve days of Christmas beginning on Christmas Day and ending on the Twelfth Night with a large party that included lots of different foods. The presentation of the boar's head was common at these gatherings. Christians in Europe believed that the serving of the beast's noggin symbolized the triumph of the Christ Child over sin.

It was usually served with a drink known as wassail that was a hot, spiced punch. It was said that Martin greatly enjoyed dining on the boar's head.

After Christmas 1831 and with a belly full of English food and drink, Martin began dropping hints to President Andrew Jackson about becoming his next vice president. It was part of his master plan to serve one term as vice president, and then run for president in 1836. After giving the matter some thought, Jackson approved the idea and Martin Van Buren became the new vice president.

In 1835, Vice President Van Buren became the center of attention at that year's White House Christmas party. He played a game of tag with the kids but lost. According to the rules, he then had to shout, "Here I stand all ragged and dirty, if you don't kiss me I'll run like a turkey." Since nobody kissed him, he did a turkey dance!

Just as he had planned, Martin ran for president in 1836 and won. Since he had never remarried, he needed someone to take care of all of the activities at the mansion. That responsibility was taken over by his daughter-in-law Sarah Van Buren who was just twenty years old. She was the youngest woman ever to hold the title of First Lady and was also in charge of the annual White House Christmas party.

Many do not realize that it was President Van Buren who chose the color and furniture of the White House's famous Blue Room, which is the place where the mansion's official Christmas tree stands during the holiday season. It is one of the most famous places in the historic house.

There was also a connection to the holidays among those who served in the Van Buren administration. Joel Poinsett was the Secretary of War but he is best remembered as the man who, a few years earlier, sent the first poinsettias to the United States from Mexico while serving as an ambassador.

For those who believe that their lucky number is eight, then Martin Van Buren might be one of their favorite people. He was elected the eighth president of the United States and was also the eighth vice president. He served eight months as U.S. Minister to England. In 1838, President Van Buren's image appeared on the eight-cent postage stamp and his wife Hannah was born on March . . . yes, you guessed it . . . the eighth!

Today's Questions

1. What country did Martin Van Buren's ancestors leave to come to America?
2. What did Martin Van Buren eat when he celebrated Christmas in England?
3. What is the color of the famous room in the White House chosen by Martin Van Buren?

It's a Fact . . .

Two major events took place in 1836—Martin Van Buren was elected president of the United States and Alabama became the first state to make Christmas an official holiday. After that, Louisiana and Arkansas followed in 1838.

Yes, it's true!

An image of President Tyler hosting an event for children at the White House (public domain).

Chapter 9

John Tyler
The 10th President
Waiting for Julia

Most people who get married can remember where they first met. For President John Tyler, the holidays of 1842 were a special time. That's because that is when he fell in love with his future wife.

That year, the nation's leader gave a small Christmas Eve party at the White House. Among those who were invited were the Gardiner family of New York which included their twenty-two-year-old daughter Julia. That evening, she was in the same room with the president during the festivities but interestingly, the two of them never spoke to each other.

However, that changed one week later when Julia returned to the mansion for a New Year's get together. During that time, she and President Tyler talked and got to know one another. Even though he was quite a bit older than she (thirty years) as time passed, they began to fall in love.

But trying to make Julia his wife proved to be challenging for the nation's leader. The first time that he proposed marriage to her was on George Washington's birthday in 1843 and she turned him down. However, he didn't give up, and once again asked her to marry him just one month later. But the answer was the same as before—no!

In just a matter of weeks, Julia had turned down the offer to marry the president of the United States—not just once, but twice!

President Tyler, who had served as a soldier in the War of 1812 and knew a thing or two about being patient, refused to give up. The members of his family celebrated Christmas 1843 in Washington, D.C., but Julia remained with Gardiners in New York. However, they got together in the spring of 1844, over a year after he first proposed to her, and Julia finally consented to become the president's wife.

In June 1844, the couple was married in New York City. They left office in March 1845 and moved to the Tyler plantation at Charles City, Virginia, where they went on to have seven children.

Today's Questions

1. What state was the home of Julia Gardiner? New Hampshire, New Jersey, or New York?
2. Whose birthday was it the first time that President Tyler proposed to Julia?
3. Where did President Tyler and Julia get married?

It's a Fact . . .

In 1843, while John Tyler was president, the first Christmas card went on sale. It was sold in London, England, by John Callcott Horsley and did not include a picture of Santa Claus.
   Yes, it's true!

CHAPTER 10

James K. Polk
The 11th President
The Christmas Wedding

Many people don't have to work on Christmas Day. They receive the time off to be with their families. However, there are people who have certain jobs that do have to work on Christmas. Those include doctors and nurses at hospitals; police officers; and members of the military. Do you know someone who has had to work on Christmas Day?

You might not have known it, but the president of the United States not only works on Christmas but every other day as well. They must always be ready to handle an emergency even if they are away from the White House.

James K. Polk was the eleventh president and served from 1845 to 1849. This was a very busy time in the nation's history and didn't allow many chances for parties or vacations.

Among the events that kept the nation's leader busy was from 1846 to 1848 when the United States was at war with Mexico; the issue of slavery in several states; and the addition of three new states (Texas, Iowa, and Wisconsin) along with other territories that wanted to join the country.

The president kept a diary which is a book where he wrote down the events that took place each day. On Christmas in 1848, his last as president, Mr. Polk wrote that his wife and children attended church but never mentioned a celebration being held that day. He simply stated that it was, "perhaps the most quiet day of my Presidential term."

Even though he didn't host any large White House holiday get togethers, President Polk had an important connection to that time of year through his parents. It was their wedding day.

On Christmas Day in 1794, Samuel Polk married Jane Knox in North Carolina. Eleven months later, their son James was born. He was the first of their ten children. It was not unusual in those days for families to have a large number of kids.

When James was ten years old, the family moved to Tennessee to join his grandfather who owned thousands of acres of land. It was a difficult journey for the Polks who traveled nearly five hundred miles by wagon. After that, it took a great deal of hard work to clear the land and build a home.

Years later when he was living in the White House, President Polk was so busy taking care of the country that he never had a chance to enjoy Christmas like other presidents had done. But he would always remember that it was the day that his parents began their life together.

For those who were mailing Christmas cards in 1847, while James K. Polk was president, the first official U.S. postage stamps were issued. The five-cent stamp picturing Benjamin Franklin (left) was for letter delivery under 300 miles. The ten-cent stamp honoring George Washington (right) was for those traveling more than 300 miles. Mail going from the east to the Pacific Coast cost the sender forty cents (public domain).

TODAY'S QUESTIONS

1. Can you name a job where people must go to work on Christmas Day?

2. While James K. Polk was president, the United States was at war with this country.
   (A) England   (B) Mexico   (C) Canada
3. Who got married on Christmas Day in 1794?

It's a Fact . . .

Many people send Christmas cards each year to friends and family members. Those envelopes always require a stamp if they are mailed. The first official U.S. postage stamps were issued in 1847, during James K. Polk's term as president.
   Yes, it's true!

General Zachary Taylor shortly before he became president (public domain).

Chapter 11

Zachary Taylor
The 12th President
Christmas in Many Places

The year of 1848 was a special one for General Zachary Taylor because some important things happened to him. First of all, he retired from his career in the military after spending forty years with the U.S. Army. Over that period, he fought in four wars and lived in a number of different places.

Soldiers are often required to move around a great deal because of the demands of their job. That was true for General Taylor who, even though his wife and children were always with him, rarely got to stay in one area for more than a brief time. Surprisingly, he never even lived in one place long enough to register to vote. The first time that he voted was when he was sixty-two years old! Do you know anyone who has ever voted in an election?

All of those moves also meant that Christmas was celebrated in many different places. Sometimes, he wasn't able to enjoy the holiday at all like in 1837 when the general was commanding troops in Florida.

That year on Christmas Day, he and his men were fighting and winning against the Seminole Indians in one of the biggest battles with a Native American tribe during the nineteenth century. In 1840, he moved his family to a new home that he had bought in Louisiana.

When his military career came to end in 1848, Taylor didn't have to wait very long to begin a new job. That November, he was elected president of the United States. That was the election where he voted for the first time. Perhaps he was meant to be the leader of the country because his cousin was former president James Madison.

He was sworn into office in March 1849 but his term was short. After just seventeen months in office, the president died of natural causes. That meant that the Christmas of 1849 would be the only one that the Taylors would celebrate at the White House.

Although her daughter Betty Bliss served as the official hostess for most of the events at the mansion, First Lady Peggy Taylor was in charge of the Christmas festivities that year. They welcomed relatives who were visiting from Maryland, Louisiana, Mississippi, Virginia, and Kentucky who joined them for the holidays.

The First Lady kept busy serving her favorite dessert to her guests. It was old-fashioned coconut cakes which was a tradition in the south where she had grown up.

Although the Taylors celebrated only one Christmas at the White House, it was truly a joyous family get-together.

Today's Questions

1. How many years was Zachary Taylor in the army? 20, 30, or 40?
2. What was Betty Bliss's job at the White House?
3. What was First Lady Peggy Taylor's favorite dessert?

It's a Fact . . .

On Christmas Eve 1849, while the First Family and their guests were gathering at the White House, on the other side of the country, many citizens were scurrying to save their lives and property. On that morning, a major fire broke out in the area known as Portsmouth Square in San Francisco, California.

About fifty buildings were destroyed as volunteers did what they could to fight the blaze. Two days later, San Francisco's city council passed a resolution to organize its own fire department.

Yes, it's true!

Chapter 12

Millard Fillmore
The 13th President
Together Again

In 1837, Millard Fillmore was elected to Congress. It meant that he would be moving to Washington, D.C., while his wife and children remained in their hometown of Buffalo, New York, which was more than 300 miles away. As many families use Christmastime to gather together, the Congressman's new position was the beginning of a period when the Fillmores were separated during the holiday season for several years.

However, Fillmore returned to Buffalo and his family in 1843 where he worked at other jobs in the government and education for the next few years. It gave him a chance to watch his young children grow up and to be with them at Christmas.

In 1848, he was elected the nation's vice president requiring him to return to the nation's capital. But little did he know that when Zachary Taylor died in 1850, and he became the new president, the event would bring his family back together again. His wife Abigail; their seventeen-year-old daughter Abby; and twenty-one-year-old son Powers also found themselves moving to Washington, D.C., to join together at their new home, the White House.

Powers had graduated from college where he studied law. When his father became president, he served as his personal assistant.

Abby was a musician who played the piano, harp, and guitar. She quit her job as a teacher to become the official White House hostess. It meant that she would be in charge of all of the mansion's Christmas celebrations.

President Fillmore's most eventful Christmas Eve took place in 1851. That evening, he, along with several members of his cabinet, rushed across town to help put out a fire at the Library of Congress. The cabinet is a group of top officials who are in charge of the government's departments such as the Secretary of the Treasury.

Since there was no equipment like firemen have today, the group formed a "bucket brigade" to help put out the flames. They passed pales of water, one after another, but the flames didn't completely die out until Christmas Day.

The president was a lover of books and had created the first library in the White House. He was sad when told that about two-thirds of the Library of Congress' books had been destroyed in the blaze. Two weeks later, a plan was approved by the elected officials in the House of Representatives to repair and enlarge the Library using fireproof materials.

Since then, it has become the largest collection of book material in the world, with more than 118 million items located on more than 500 miles of shelves. The book that you are currently reading is one of them!

When Millard Fillmore became president, he knew that his job would be to lead the nation. But he also received a true gift which was that he had his family together again.

The main Reading Room at the Library of Congress as it looks today (public domain photo).

Today's Questions

1. What was the name of Millard Fillmore's hometown?
2. Abby Fillmore quit her job as a teacher for another job. What was her new position?
3. Where did the big fire take place on Christmas Eve of 1851?

It's a Fact . . .

While Millard Fillmore was president, Mark Carr started the country's first Christmas tree market. In 1851, he cut down fir and spruce trees that were growing wild in the Catskill Mountains of Upstate New York. Mr. Carr loaded two oxcarts with trees and took them by ship to New York City.

He rented some space where he sold them for one dollar each. The local citizens quickly bought up his entire supply. That year started a successful business for the Carr family that lasted until 1898.

Yes, it's true!

President Franklin Pierce greets a group of guests at the White House (public domain).

CHAPTER 13

Franklin Pierce
The 14th President
The First Christmas Tress

One of the traditions of the holiday season is the Christmas tree. Like most items in our lives, there is a history behind it.

Before America was discovered, citizens in parts of Europe were already celebrating the season with evergreen trees. But when the Pilgrims arrived at Plymouth in the 1620s, their governor William Bradford, told his followers that there would be no celebrating because it would interfere with their work. That meant no exchanging of gifts or a special meal like we enjoy today.

In 1659, the lawmakers of Massachusetts officially disallowed the recognition of Christmas. Anyone found breaking the new law was fined. But as time passed, and more Europeans came to America, Christmas was not only celebrated but many of their customs became a part of it.

One of the most important was the Christmas tree. They began being displayed in the 1830s by the German settlers of Pennsylvania. Over the years, people began decorating their trees with handmade ornaments and foods like popcorn. Other items like holly and pine cones were also used as decorations.

While much is known about the Christmas tree in the United States, some continue to wonder which president had the first one at the White House? There are those who believe it was Franklin Pierce.

He was elected in 1852 and came from New Hampshire. While it's a small state, it's a place that is known for growing a large number of Christmas trees.

It was said that in 1856, President Pierce decorated one of the small trees growing outside of the mansion for a group of children from a

Washington, D.C., Sunday school as caroler's sang "Hark, the Herald Angels Sing."

Today, there are many types of Christmas trees. Some are living while others are made of plastic or other materials. Modern-day trees may be larger and more colorful but they got their start many years ago when America was just beginning to become a country.

Today's Questions

1. William Bradford told this group that they were not allowed to celebrate Christmas. Who were they?
2. They were the people who introduced the Christmas tree to America. Was it the Germans or the Dutch?
3. Where was the Christmas tree that President Franklin Pierce decorated for the children from the Sunday school?

It's a Fact . . .

There are many well-known Christmas songs. One of the most popular is "I Heard the Bells on Christmas Day." The words were written in 1863 by the famous poet, Henry Wadsworth Longfellow.

He and President Franklin Pierce got to know each other in college and remained friends for life.

Yes, it's true!

Chapter 14

James Buchanan
The 15th President
A Divided Christmas

Being the president of the United States is a very difficult job as an important part of it is to keep the country safe. In 1860, that proved to be a tough task for President James Buchanan.

Slavery was the issue that threatened to divide the nation as the northern states wanted to do away with it while the southern states were in favor of keeping it in their areas. For President Buchanan, he had to do what was best for all of the people, not just those who lived in a certain part of the country.

The southern states believed that it was their right to have or not have slaves. It meant that cotton and tobacco farmers could make more money because they didn't have to pay the slaves to tend the crops. Some were able to escape but most of them remained on the plantations where they worked for long hours.

The problem worsened just five days before Christmas in 1860 when South Carolina announced that they would no longer be a part of the United States. After all of the sacrifices to build the states into one nation, the country was now faced with several of them pulling out. When a state leaves its country, it is called secession (pronounced see-cesh-on).

President Buchanan was from the north and had always been against slavery. Twice, he became a sort of Santa Claus giving some of them the gift of freedom. On those occasions, he purchased several slaves, took them north, and later set them free in his home state of Pennsylvania.

Even though he was only able to help a few of the slaves, it brought joy to their lives. However, following the Christmas holidays, ten other southern states joined South Carolina and left the nation.

The Christmas season of 1860 was a lonely one for President Buchanan as he had no wife or children to share the holidays while he desperately tried to keep the nation together. Three months later, Abraham Lincoln replaced him as president and he returned home to Pennsylvania.

Sometimes, the Christmas season isn't a happy time for all but a few years afterward, all of the slaves gained their freedom and they were able to celebrate the holidays as citizens of the United States.

A group of slaves working in the cotton field looking for freedom (public domain).

TODAY'S QUESTIONS

1. What is secession?
2. Why did South Carolina leave the United States?
3. Who bought slaves and released them in Pennsylvania?

IT'S A FACT . . .

In December 1860, President Buchanan invited a group of Pawnee Indians to the White House for a Christmas party. The U.S. government had signed a treaty with the tribe about two years earlier.

Yes, it's true!

Chapter 15

Abraham Lincoln
The 16th President
The Soldiers and Christmas

Abraham Lincoln was the president of the United States from 1861 to 1865, which meant that he celebrated four Christmases while serving as the nation's leader. All of these took place during the Civil War.

The war was fought between the northern and southern states. The main reason for the fighting was slavery. Here's some information on each of the four Christmases that Abraham Lincoln celebrated as president.

The afternoon of Christmas 1861 was like any other day for President Lincoln. He worked in his office, took part in some meetings, and checked on the progress of the northern troops who were fighting in the war.

Meanwhile, Mrs. Lincoln read books and helped serve meals to wounded soldiers at two different hospitals. She had raised a thousand dollars to help pay for the Christmas dinners and also donated citrus fruit to the men to prevent scurvy, a disease caused by a lack of vitamin C in a person's diet.

That evening, the Lincolns hosted a dinner party at the White House with many family and friends who were visiting from Illinois and Kentucky.

The following year, the Lincolns spent Christmas Day visiting soldiers at hospitals in Washington, D.C. Meanwhile, southern troops were busy destroying a railroad line in Kentucky. The railroads were very important during the war for transporting men and supplies.

That same day in Hilton Head, South Carolina, northern soldiers were relaxing by playing a game of a new sport called baseball.

During the Christmas season of 1863, the president brought his son Tad to the hospitals to visit the wounded soldiers. After seeing them, the nine-year-old boy wanted to do something to help and asked his father if he could send books and clothing as gifts. President Lincoln was moved and gave his approval. Shortly afterward, soldiers began receiving packages for Christmas signed, "From Tad Lincoln."

By the time that the holidays arrived in 1864, the north was close to winning the war. The president received a message with some good news from one of his top generals William T. Sherman which said, "I beg to present you, as a Christmas gift, the city of Savannah...."

The capture of this Georgia city was important for the north and made Mr. Lincoln very happy.

But the taking of Savannah did include a Christmas story of giving. Following the capture, ninety northern soldiers and their captain took several wagons of food and supplies and gave them away to local citizens. The people were thankful and watched when the empty wagons left being pulled by mules that had been decorated with reindeer antlers made from small tree branches.

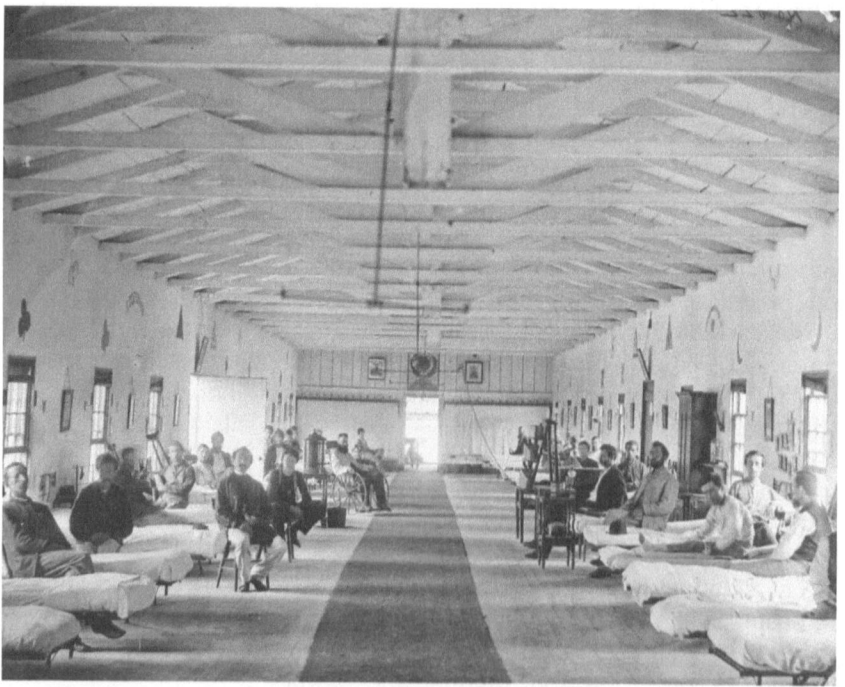

The Lincolns often visited soldiers at Armory Square Hospital in Washington, D.C., especially at Christmas time (Library of Congress photo).

Four months later, the war was finished and slavery was officially over in America. The soldiers went home to their families and were able to celebrate the Christmas of 1865 with loved ones as one nation.

Today's Questions

1. What was the name of the war that was fought over slavery?
2. Why did Mrs. Lincoln raise $1,000?
3. What did the soldiers use for reindeer antlers on their mules?

It's a Fact . . .

On Christmas Day 1864, Tad Lincoln befriended several hungry children and invited them to attend Christmas dinner at the White House with his family. President Lincoln welcomed the young guests who enjoyed a special holiday meal with the leader of the country.
    Yes, it's true!

Christmas letters that get mailed to Santa Claus are delivered to the post office at the town of North Pole in Alaska (Image courtesy of Paul Brown, Operations Manager, Santa Claus House).

Chapter 16

Andrew Johnson
The 17th President
A Christmas Pardon

Anyone who thought that the job of president of the United States would become easy once the war ended was mistaken. There was still a great deal of work to do and that responsibility fell upon the shoulders of the nation's new leader, Andrew Johnson.

By Christmas 1868, the Civil War had been over for more than three years but that didn't matter to a number of people who were still angry. They were mad at the Americans who had fought for the south and believed that they needed to be punished.

One of the powers of the president is the ability to issue pardons. A pardon is an official document that forgives individuals who have committed serious crimes without having to serve a penalty like going to prison. President Johnson, who had been born and raised in the south, was faced with the choice of whether or not to penalize those who had fought against the north.

In May 1865, he granted pardons to all white Southerners except the government leaders. This meant that those who served in the southern army wouldn't be charged with any war crimes. The decision upset many northerners who didn't agree with the president's decision.

In July 1868, President Johnson issued a second pardon that applied to most of the southern government's officials and their army officers. Once again, a large number of citizens were angry at their leader. They were so upset that Mr. Johnson wasn't nominated to run for another term.

It meant that the president had one last decision to make. Should he issue a final pardon for all of the remaining members of the southern government and military? He knew that if he did, it would make more citizens turn against him.

What would you do?

President Johnson was faced with an important task to bring the nation together again as one. No more north and south, no more slavery, just one United States of America. This was the challenge that faced him.

On Christmas Day 1868, President Johnson issued a final pardon for the southerners who had not been included in the first two orders. One of those who was forgiven for his actions in that last pardon was Alexander Stephens who had been the vice president of the southern states. For those who were pardoned on that day, they could not have received a better Christmas present.

Three months later, in March 1869, Andrew Johnson left the White House as president for the last time. Some people were still not happy with his actions but as the years passed, citizens of the north and south buried their differences and, once again, became united as one country just as they had before the Civil War.

TODAY'S QUESTIONS

1. Who was the president who issued the three important pardons following the Civil War?
2. True or false—All of the citizens agreed with the president's decision to issue the pardons.
3. What holiday was being celebrated when the president issued the third pardon?

IT'S A FACT . . .

On March 30, 1867, while Andrew Johnson was president, the United States reached an agreement to purchase the territory of Alaska from Russia for $7.2 million. In 1959, it became the forty-ninth state.

In case you were wondering where all those letters go that get mailed to Santa Claus, they are delivered to the post office at the town of North Pole in Alaska!

Yes, it's true!

Chapter 17

Ulysses S. Grant
The 18th President
An Official Holiday

Ulysses S. Grant became one of the most famous men of the 1800s. He was the winning general of the Civil War and then served two terms as president of the United States. The soldier was also a national hero but it wasn't always that way. He overcame hardships along his path to become well known.

In the 1850s, after serving eleven years in the army, Grant and his wife started a farm in Missouri but they had a difficult time and it didn't do well. In fact, in 1857, he was forced to sell his gold pocket watch for $22 in order to buy Christmas presents for his family. A few weeks later, the ex-soldier was stricken with the deadly disease malaria. There was no doubt about it, things were going badly.

When the Civil War broke out in 1861, Grant rejoined the army and his life, along with his luck, began to change. That same year President Lincoln promoted him to be a general in the northern military. Over the next four years, his men battled the southern troops at many places. Sometimes, his family would be able to visit him where he was stationed.

However, General Grant's wife Julia and their son Jesse had a close call just a few days before Christmas in 1862. They had traveled to Holly Springs in Mississippi for a visit with the general when the town was raided by southern soldiers. The troops went to the house where Julia and Jesse had been staying but they had already left the area. That Christmas proved to be lucky for the Grant family.

Over the following months, General Grant's soldiers won several important battles. President Lincoln was so impressed that he appointed him as his top general for all of the northern troops. By the spring of 1865, the north had defeated the south and Grant was hailed as a hero.

After the war, the general received many honors. One of those was having a giant sequoia tree named after him at Kings Canyon National Park in California. It is believed to be nearly 3,000 years old, stands 267 feet tall, and nearly 29 feet wide at the base making it the second largest in the world. In 1926, the massive sequoia was officially declared as the nation's Christmas tree.

In 1869, Ulysses S. Grant became the eighteenth president of the United States. That Christmas, the family hosted their first White House Christmas party ever to be reported in a local newspaper. The story gave the names of the guests, details about the dinner and the activities that were held after the meal. It was the first time that citizens could read the news and learn about the events that took place at the mansion's big Christmas gathering.

On June 28, 1870, President Grant signed a bill that made many people happy. It declared that New Year's Day, the fourth of July, Thanksgiving Day along with Christmas would all become national holidays. That meant that many workers would have time off from their jobs to celebrate those special days with their families.

The following year, John Clem dropped by the White House on Christmas Day. He had served under Mr. Grant during the Civil War when he was just ten years old. On this day, he thanked the president for his army promotion to second lieutenant. Clem eventually became a general.

Some other holiday events included the first ruling king to visit the White House arriving for Christmas 1874 when King David Kalakaua of Hawaii was a guest. He brought along his royal food testers who sampled the items served to the king. This was many years before Hawaii became a U.S. state.

In 1876, it is believed that Julia Grant became the first First Lady to send someone a Christmas card. It was received by her friend Mrs. Childs in Philadelphia.

During the Christmas season the Grants would have large wooden barrels filled with candied fruit delivered by horse drawn wagons to orphanages, old age homes, and hospitals in Washington, D.C. Mrs. Grant was also known for buying toys for poor children.

After serving two terms as president, the Grants moved to New York City where they would celebrate many more Christmases. The old general had been through some tough times during his past but in the end, he helped the United States recognize the Christmas season as its most popular holiday of the year.

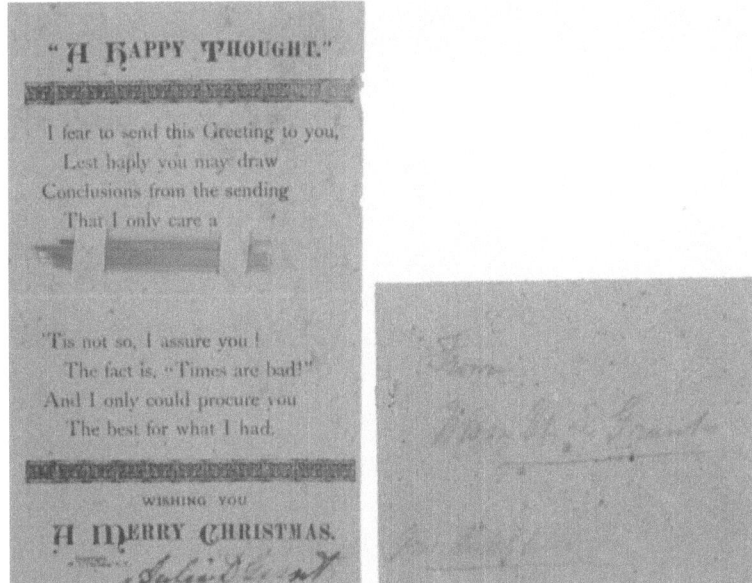

This is believed to be the first ever White House Christmas card. It was sent by Julia Grant (public domain).

Today's Questions

1. What did Ulysses S. Grant sell so that he could buy Christmas gifts for his family?
2. It is believed that Mrs. Grant sent one of these to a friend in 1876.
3. In 1874, King Kalakaua was a Christmas guest at the White House. Where was he from?

It's a Fact . . .

While Ulysses S. Grant was president, the first American to print and sell Christmas cards was Louis Prang of Roxbury, Massachusetts who began publishing them in 1875.

Yes, it's true!

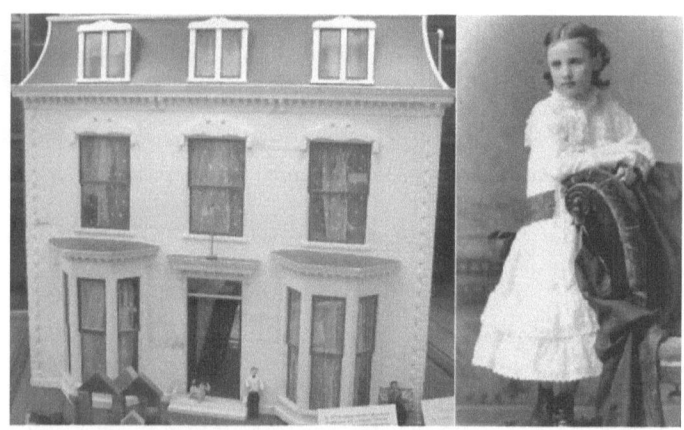

Frances Hayes (right) and the dollhouse that she received for Christmas 1877 (Hayes Presidential Center photos)

CHAPTER 18

Rutherford B. Hayes
The 19th President
Sharing Christmas Cheer

Rutherford B. Hayes became president of the United States in 1877. He was from Ohio and had five children in his family when he moved to Washington, D.C.

The holiday season was always special for Rutherford and Lucy Hayes for many reasons. The couple had been married on December 30, 1852, just five days after Christmas. She became the first First Lady to graduate from college because most women didn't attend higher education classes during that era.

Hayes was one of several men that became president who had fought in the Civil War. He was a true hero having been wounded in four different battles and, like Ulysses S. Grant, he was eventually promoted to the rank of general.

The war was difficult for soldiers since they were separated from their families. General Hayes sent letters to Lucy who was busy raising their children back at their home in Ohio. She also took time to volunteer as a nurse at a local military hospital.

Just before Christmas in 1861, Hayes, who was a Major at the time, was stationed with his troops in western Virginia when he received a telegram with good news from home announcing the birth of his new son, Joseph. The following year, he shared Christmas dinner with four of Lucy's cousins at his camp.

Years later, when he was president, the family continued to celebrate Christmas in special ways after he became president. Lucy invited members of the White House staff along with their families to join the Hayes on Christmas morning and to share a holiday meal. Some of the

African Americans who worked in the White House had been raised by parents who had been slaves so to be able to enjoy the holiday with the First Family in the mansion was truly something special.

The cheerful get-togethers would have sing-a-longs featuring Christmas carols. Among the gifts that were given that year was a hand-made dollhouse from the president and First Lady to their ten-year-old daughter Frances.

During the 1877 holiday season, the family received the first Christmas card ever sent to the White House. It was from Louis Prang in Massachusetts, the man who created the item two years earlier. While President Hayes did not send out Christmas cards, he was known for writing personal letters to friends and family during the holidays. Meanwhile, Lucy Hayes helped bring some seasonal cheer as she continued with her charity work for military veterans and orphans.

In 1878, the president's wife invited the two teenage daughters of a family friend, John Herron, to stay at the White House during the holiday. The oldest girl, seventeen-year-old Helen dreamed that she would someday return to the mansion as First Lady which she did in 1909, as the wife of President William Howard Taft.

The Hayes's last Christmas at the White House was in 1880. They spent time in the library and opened their presents in the Red Room. That year, the president presented a special gift of a $5.00 gold piece to every member of the staff.

When Rutherford B. Hayes ran for president in 1876, he promised if he won that he would serve just one term. He kept his word to the people and didn't run for reelection. A few weeks after Christmas 1880, he and his family returned to their home in Ohio but for the members of the White House staff, they would never forget the First Family's kindness.

Today's Questions

1. Lucy Hayes did something special that had never been done by another First Lady. What was it?
2. What did Frances receive as a Christmas gift from her parents?
3. What did President Hayes give to each member of his staff at their final White House Christmas?

It's a Fact . . .

Today, there are many telephones inside the White House. But the first one was installed in 1877 for President Hayes. He is not believed to have made any calls on Christmas Day.

Yes, it's true!

CHAPTER 19

Chester Arthur
The 21st President
Nell's Helping Hands

Chester Arthur became the twenty-first president of the United States in 1881. He moved into the White House with his two children: seventeen-year-old Chester II, also known as Alan, and his ten-year-old daughter Nell. Their mother had passed away a year earlier. In her absence, the president's sister Molly McElroy served as his hostess for official gatherings.

President Arthur was from New York City and was accustomed to living well in a nice home with fine furniture. So, not long after moving into the eighty-one-year-old mansion, he ordered it to be remodeled. The first duty for the staff was to remove twenty-four wagonloads of furnishings. The pieces were placed in a warehouse and eventually sold.

While her father was busy with the work going on at the White House, young Nell was focused on her own project. She helped create the St. John's Guild of the Holy Child. It was an organization that would provide hot meals on Christmas Eve and Christmas Day for thousands of local children who lived in poverty in the nation's capital. Each holiday season thereafter, she served food and also put together a drive collecting clothes and toys so that the children would have gifts for Christmas.

As the White House remodeling continued, President Arthur lived in the Cottage at the Soldiers' Home. It was a place started in 1851 as a hospital for old and disabled veterans. The Home served as the summer residence for other U.S. presidents including Abraham Lincoln, Rutherford B. Hayes, James Buchanan, as well as Chester Arthur. Although it's located just four miles from the White House, the summer temperatures were usually cooler and more comfortable. Today, the Soldiers' Home is a national historic landmark where tourists can visit.

For Christmas 1883, President Arthur received six gold-headed canes as gifts which would come in handy when he would take one of his late night walks, that he was known to do, around Washington, D.C. In turn, he gave Nell, a pair of diamond earrings and Alan, a gift of $150 in cash. Each member of the White House staff received a turkey along with a holiday bonus of $15.

Nell continued helping children in need. That Christmas, she supervised a dinner for 500 youngsters. Word of Nell's good work spread

The first Christmas tree with electric lights created by Edward H. Johnson (public domain).

throughout the capital city and other teenagers joined Christmas clubs in order to give aid to the less fortunate.

The following year (1884) was Chester Arthur's last Christmas as president. He and Alan took a sleigh ride through Washington, D.C. While, once again, Nell served dinner to the children. The men then traveled to the home of the Secretary of State where they had dinner and opened gifts with his family.

The president received several gold and silver-headed umbrellas while he gave each of the White House servants a five-dollar gold piece.

In March 1885, Chester Arthur's term as president was over and he returned to New York City. But perhaps it was the lessons of giving to others by his daughter Nell that the people remembered the most whenever the holiday season returned.

Today's Questions

1. What did President Arthur do to the White House shortly after he moved into it?
2. What was the Soldiers' Home?
3. What did Nell do on Christmas Day?

It's a Fact . . .

For years, people had used candles as lights for their Christmas trees. It was very dangerous and often led to many trees and homes catching fire.

In 1882, while Chester Arthur was president, Edward H. Johnson put together the very first string of electric Christmas tree lights. He hand-wired eighty red, white, and blue light bulbs and wound them around his revolving Christmas tree making it safer to celebrate the holiday.

How did Mr. Johnson know so much about electric lights? He worked for the man who invented them—Thomas Edison.

Yes, it's true!

A Cleveland family Christmas tree with electric lights (public domain).

Chapter 20

Grover Cleveland
The 22nd and 24th President
Holiday Changes

Grover Cleveland was just one man but he was the twenty-second and twenty-fourth president. How can that be? It's actually pretty simple.

He won the election of 1884 but lost four years later. He then returned to office when he was reelected in 1892. Grover Cleveland is the only president to serve two nonconsecutive terms as president. However, just like other two-term leaders, he enjoyed eight Christmases as the country's chief executive although his first one wasn't the happiest of holidays.

President Cleveland's first White House Christmas was in 1885. His vice president, Thomas Hendricks, had died a month earlier and he chose not to replace him. Cleveland was also a bachelor and even though he was engaged to be married, he didn't have a family or a Christmas tree that year. There were a few members of the White House staff working at the mansion that day but, after that, things began to change.

On June 2, 1886, President Cleveland married Frances Folsom at the White House. Although there have been other weddings held there, to this day, he is the only president to be married at the mansion. At age twenty-one, Frances became the nation's youngest First Lady. As one might expect, with a new wife, there were changes from the past especially during the holidays.

The Clevelands spent their first Christmas together at their farm near Washington, D.C. It was called Red Top, and Frances had decorated the home with traditional English holly and evergreens. It also included something that had not been in the White House the year before, a Christmas tree. That afternoon, they had dinner with her mother.

Each member of the staff received a letter personally written to them by the president which contained money as their gift. Like President Arthur's daughter Nell had done, Mrs. Cleveland worked with local charities that provided Christmas dinners for the poor children of Washington.

During her years as First Lady, Frances preferred providing food, clothing, and toys to the disadvantaged rather than planning or entertaining at the White House. She would often buy gifts and then wrap and distribute them herself. The First Lady was also an active member of the Colored Christmas Club that helped African American youngsters.

In 1887, the Clevelands enjoyed Christmas dinner at the White House which included Oysters on the Half Shell; Game Soup; Broiled White Fish; Roast Goose; Boiled Potatoes; Mashed Turnips; Christmas Plum Pudding; Vanilla Ice Cream; and Mince Pie. But the following year (1888) wasn't so merry. President Cleveland was defeated for reelection and a few weeks later, they moved to New York City where he worked as a lawyer.

When the Clevelands returned to the White House after winning the election of 1892, two things were different. Their daughter Ruth had been born in 1891 and another daughter Esther arrived in the fall of 1893. She was the first child of a president born in the White House.

In 1893, shortly after Esther was born, Frances returned to her role of working with poor children as she helped organize a holiday party. Toys and candy were given to the kids which was followed by Christmas dinner and a puppet show. The First Lady had been away from Washington, D.C., for four years but when she returned, everyone could tell that she hadn't changed. Frances was still the kind and loving person that they had known during the president's first term in office.

Christmas in 1894 would be a history-making event. That year, the first electric lights on a First Family tree were used. That fact was pretty amazing because electricity had only been used in the White House for three years. The president gave each member of his cabinet a duck for Christmas dinner that he had bagged during a recent hunting trip to South Carolina.

The Clevelands welcomed their third daughter, Marion, to the family in 1895. That holiday season, the president had the staff decorate the Christmas tree with hundreds of multicolored electric light bulbs. It also had gold angels with spreading wings, gold and silver sleds, and lots of tinsel. All of the daughters received gifts. Among them, Esther was given a miniature White House for her dolls.

The Clevelands's last White House Christmas was in 1896, and it was spectacular. It featured a twenty-foot beautifully decorated Christmas tree in the library while the main course at dinner was a fifty-seven pound turkey! Meanwhile, the president preformed the tradition of hanging stockings on the fireplace mantel that were stuffed with candy, figs, and toys.

At the end of his second term, the Clevelands returned to New York where they completed their family with the birth of two sons. While Grover Cleveland was president, the country grew larger adding another state (Utah). The White House Christmas celebrations also grew but there would be more surprises to come!

Today's Questions

1. During his first Christmas at the White House, President Cleveland didn't have one of these. What was it?
2. Where did President Cleveland marry Frances? Here's a hint, their daughter Esther was born there.
3. The Clevelands were the first to have these on their White House Christmas tree. What were they?

It's a Fact . . .

Today, many professional baseball teams play their games in enclosed stadiums. However, on Christmas Day 1888, while Grover Cleveland was president, the first indoor baseball game was played.

It took place at the state fairgrounds in Philadelphia, Pennsylvania, inside a large building. A team called the Uptowners beat the Downtowners 6-1 in front of a crowd of about 2,000 curious fans.

The idea has grown as there are currently six big league teams that have roofs on their stadiums.

Yes, it's true!

President Benjamin Harrison's grandchildren rode in a cart on the South Lawn of the White House pulled by their pet goat, "His Whiskers" (Photo by Frances Benjamin Johnston, courtesy Library of Congress).

Chapter 21

Benjamin Harrison
The 23rd President
The President with the White Beard

Christmas was a special day for Benjamin Harrison who became president in March 1889. That was understandable since he, like another famous fellow, sported a white beard.

The president's first White House Christmas was quite an event. At 10:00 am on December 25, 1889, Mary Dimmick, the niece of First Lady Caroline Harrison, tooted a toy horn to notify everyone that it was time for the Christmas celebration to begin. That would feature a large gathering that included Caroline's father, the First Couple's two grown children and their families, all of whom had moved into the mansion when Benjamin became president.

But the nation's leader's pride and joy were his three small grandchildren. Their grandfather was determined to make their first White House Christmas very special. On Christmas Eve, the president's children Mamie and Russell set about decorating the indoor White House Christmas tree. It had glass ornaments, toy soldiers, and candles. Gifts were laid below the base and in some of the branches. The First Lady, who was an artist, had planned how the tree would be presented.

For the first time, it was set up in the Yellow Room on the second floor which served as a library and parlor. After breakfast, the family gathered around to light the tree's candles.

President Harrison's young grandchildren, Benjamin and Mary McKee, received many fine gifts. Mary was given baby doll furniture, with several dolls, and other toys. Little Benjamin, also known as Baby McKee, received pieces to a train set, along with books and pictures.

President Harrison passed out turkeys to the White House staff. In turn, he received a silver dollar-shaped picture holder from his daughter, Mamie. Russell presented his mother with a new piano. As usual, the president received a number of gifts from citizens including a group in Utah who sent him a crate of extra-large potatoes, most weighing over three pounds each.

Dinner was served at 4:00 pm featuring oysters, turtle stew, roast turkey with cranberry jelly, vegetables, fruits, with many different desserts including pies and ice cream. It had been a very special Christmas Day.

Two years later, in 1891, there was another bit of White House Christmas history that was made. That year, Benjamin Harrison became the first president to dress as Santa Claus. Since he wore a natural white beard, there was no need to put on the disguise. He then read "The Night before Christmas" to his family. The small grandchildren recited poems in German—taught to them by their German nanny, Fraulein Hampe.

Many of the traditions that have been celebrated during Christmas at the White House over the years began with the Harrison family.

Today's Questions

1. What did the Harrisons place in the Yellow Room of the White House that had never been there before?
2. What did President Harrison receive as a Christmas gift from some citizens in Utah?
3. Benjamin Harrison became the first president to dress up like this well-known Christmas figure. Who was it?

It's a Fact...

In 1890, while Benjamin Harrison was president, James Edgar became the first department store Santa Claus. He would stroll through his place of business in Brockton, Massachusetts spreading Christmas cheer to customers and children.

Yes, it's true!

Chapter 22

William McKinley
The 25th President
Tough Times at Christmas

Christmas is a joyous period of the year for most people. But it was a difficult time for President William McKinley and his wife Ida.

Their daughter Katie was born on Christmas Day 1871 while they were living in Ohio. The little girl brought great happiness to her parents but, unfortunately, she died in 1875 of typhoid fever. At the time, she was just three-and-a-half years old.

Typhoid is a bacterial disease that is treated with vaccines. But those medicines had not yet been created when Katie was infected.

Nonetheless, when the McKinleys moved into the White House in 1897, they did their best to make the most of the holiday season. The First Lady would often travel to New York City to shop for presents. They would sometimes welcome friends from Ohio who would spend Christmas with them at the White House.

The holiday season of 1898 was a welcome bit of relief for the McKinleys. The Spanish-American War, which had seen American troops fighting in Cuba for most of the year, had ended on December 10. When the couple attended church services in Washington, D.C., on Christmas morning, their minister Reverend Bristol called the peace treaty, "God's gift of freedom to the Cuban people."

Clara Barton, the founder of the American branch of the Red Cross, met with the president during the last week of December, to discuss how her organization could help those who were affected by the war.

Of the gifts, that year, President McKinley gave his wife two shiny diamond bracelets. But perhaps the most treasured present from her husband came the following Christmas (1899) when he gave her a blue frame studded with diamonds that surrounded a picture of their daughter Katie.

That year, the McKinleys also welcomed their five-year-old grandniece Marjorie Morse to the mansion for the first time during a holiday. In addition, a small Christmas tree was set up for her. It was the first tree of its kind to be placed in the White House during William McKinley's presidency.

But not everyone was happy with the decision. Some people feared that the harvesting of Christmas trees would ruin the nation's forests. President McKinley received one letter from an angry individual who called the cutting down of the trees, "un-American."

The president ignored the remark and that evening enjoyed pieces from a large turkey that was sent to the First Family from a farmer in Rhode Island.

The year of 1900 would mark the McKinleys fourth and final Christmas in the White House. Among the guests that year was the president's niece Mabel who was a famous opera singer.

A Christmas image of President McKinley and friend (Puck Magazine, 1900).

TODAY'S QUESTIONS

1. Where did Mrs. McKinley go to do her Christmas shopping?
2. Whose picture was in the blue frame that the president gave to his wife?

3. When their grandniece Marjorie Morse came for the holidays, the McKinleys put up something in the White House that they hadn't done before. What was it?

It's a Fact . . .

On October 30, 1899, while William McKinley was president, banjo player Will Lyle made history by recording the song "Jingle Bells." It became the first piece of Christmas music ever recorded.

Yes, it's true!

A Christmas image of President Theodore Roosevelt by W. A. Rogers from Harper's Weekly *magazine on December 14, 1901.*

Chapter 23

Theodore Roosevelt
The 26th President
Bah-Humbug!

Do you remember Ebenezer Scrooge? He was one of the main characters from Charles Dickens's wonderful story "A Christmas Carol." Whenever others tried to make him see the good things about Christmas, he would reply in a harsh tone, "Bah, humbug!"

President Theodore Roosevelt has never been compared to Scrooge. In fact, he enjoyed Christmas and celebrated it every year. But there was one tradition that he didn't want in the White House . . . a Christmas tree.

You might remember that in our last chapter there were those who disagreed with President William McKinely and his display of a tree in the White House. However, President Roosevelt was a conservationist who feared that forests would be destroyed because of the loss of pine trees. Because of that, he wouldn't allow a Christmas tree to be placed in the mansion.

Roosevelt told his family, "It's not good to cut down trees for mere decoration. We must set a good example for the people of America."

There were no problems during that first year (1901), but in 1902, the president faced a revolt from within the members of his own family. As Christmas approached, his two youngest sons, Archie and Quentin, walked around the White House grounds where they located a small tree and cut it down. Then, they quietly smuggled it into a closet of the room where the family would be opening their gifts. After hiding the tree, the boys were able to convince the White House electrician to decorate it with tiny lights that were wired to a switch outside the closet. The worker also kept their tree a secret from the boys' parents.

Can you imagine keeping a secret like that from the president of the United States?

On Christmas morning, the family, that included six children along with three of their pets (a dog, a cat, and a pony), gathered around the room to open their presents. At that point, Archie made his way to the closet, turned on the switch, and opened the door to reveal the small but professionally lit and decorated Christmas tree with gifts.

Although, he was not happy that his sons had disobeyed him, the president found it amusing and told a friend, So their mother and I got up, shut the window, lit the fire (taking down the stockings of course), put on our wrappers and prepared to admit the children. But first there was a surprise for me, also for their good mother, for Archie had a little birthday tree of his own which he had rigged up with the help of one of the carpenters in a big closet; and we all had to look at the tree and each of us got a present off of it.

However, the cutting down of the tree still bothered the president. He spoke to a friend who had been a college professor and was an expert in forestry. He told President Roosevelt that thinning the forests by cutting down Christmas trees actually helped the areas thrive by allowing new ones to grow. He was not aware of that fact and changed his mind about having a Christmas tree in the White House in the future.

Following lunch, the president, who was a former soldier and cowboy, took part in one of his favorite activities as he mounted his trusted horse for a Christmas ride. Joining the nation's leader for the holiday jaunt was his son Ted, and two other friends who took a three-hour ride through the snow.

The Roosevelts were always known for doing things in a big way, and Christmas 1903 was no exception. They hosted one of the largest holiday parties ever to be held at the White House as they welcomed 600 children of government officials as guests. They enjoyed music and refreshments with the president and First Lady who acted as host and hostess. A special Christmas dinner was served in the state dining room, the area where banquets are held for famous visitors to the mansion.

For their final White House Christmas in 1908, the First Family welcomed some fifty guests. They dined on roast turkey with vegetables for the main course. For dessert, the crowd enjoyed plum pudding with ice cream portions that were shaped like Santa Claus. There was a Christmas tree with many gifts that awaited the family's celebration. A few weeks later, the Roosevelts returned to their home in New York.

In 1918, the former president had been in the hospital due to health problems. But on Christmas morning, he left the health care unit so that he could have Christmas dinner at home with his family. He seemed to be improving but two weeks later, died suddenly at his home in Sagamore Hill, New York.

Quentin Roosevelt, the president's son who hid the Christmas tree in the White House, grew up and became a U.S. Army pilot. He died in service to his country when his plane was shot down in combat during World War I, just a few months before his father passed away.

However, there was good news that year because World War I ended in 1918 and a few days afterward, there was a ceremony to celebrate that season's White House Christmas tree. No doubt, Quentin would have been proud.

Today's Questions

1. Why wouldn't President Roosevelt allow a Christmas tree in the White House?
2. Where did Archie and Quentin hide the Christmas tree?
3. Who put the lights on Archie and Quentin's tree?

It's a Fact . . .

Have you ever owned a Teddy Bear? Were you ever curious as to how it got its name?

In November 1902, President Roosevelt was on a hunting trip in Mississippi. A story made the newspapers about how the nation's leader had refused to shoot a bear that had already been captured. He said that to do such a thing would be unsportsmanlike.

Because of the story, store owners began calling their stuffed animals, "Teddy's Bears." They were named after the president's nickname of Teddy. The name has remained and the toys are still one of the top sellers to this day especially at Christmas.

Yes, it's true!

That isn't Santa Claus riding a reindeer, it's former president William Howard Taft atop a carabao (a water buffalo) while visiting the Philippine Islands in 1914 (U.S. Army History Institute).

Chapter 24

William Howard Taft
The 27th President
Christmas Wishes Do Come True

There are two presidents in America's history who remind people of Santa Claus. The first was Benjamin Harrison because of his white beard. The other was William Howard Taft who was president from 1909 to 1913. He stood 6 feet tall and weighed 325 pounds and, like Santa, could often be seen wearing a smile on his face.

President Taft greatly enjoyed Christmas. He and his wife Helen were known for doing their own shopping with the holiday crowds. They also looked forward to receiving a package each year from Massachusetts known as "Aunt Delia's goodies." The president's aunt, Delia Torrey, would always send the family a gift of apple pies, jellies, and jams made from fruit grown on the Torrey property.

The First Family included son Robert and daughter Helen who both attended college away from Washington, D.C. The youngest child, Charles, who was eleven years old when his father took office, lived with his parents at the White House. Their Christmases were not as spectacular as the Roosevelts had been. In fact, they were usually pretty quiet as the family opened gifts in the morning and enjoyed a turkey dinner later in the day. The delicious bird usually weighed thirty to four pounds and was delivered by Horace Vose, who was known as the poultry king of Rhode Island.

However, that doesn't mean that the Tafts didn't have any excitement during the holiday season. In fact, on Christmas Eve 1911, the president and First Lady disappeared for almost two hours! They were able to leave the White House without being noticed by the Secret Service whose job it is to protect them. While they were gone, the Tafts walked around

Washington, D.C., and visited friends as their worried bodyguards tried to find them. They eventually returned safely to the mansion after having enjoyed their stroll through the capital city and the Secret Service agents could then breathe a sigh of relief.

The following year (1912), was the last winter holiday for William Howard Taft as president. However, he and the First Lady were out of the country on Christmas Day. They had traveled to the country of Panama where they were inspecting the progress of the massive canal project. That evening, the Tafts attended a ball in Panama City that was held in their honor.

The Taft children did not make the trip and remained at the White House where they created a new Christmas tradition. Robert and Helen decided to host a holiday party for some friends and relatives where they had a Christmas tree on display in the Blue Room. The popular setting became the main tree area for future holidays in the mansion and today, the main Christmas tree inside the White House is always placed in the Blue Room just as the first one was over 100 years ago by the Taft children.

TODAY'S QUESTIONS

1. What were "Aunt Delia's goodies?"
2. What was the name of the group that was looking for the Tafts when they left the White House without being noticed?
3. In what room is the main Christmas tree placed inside the White House?

IT'S A FACT . . .

Did you ever tell Santa Claus what you wanted for Christmas and then got exactly that? It actually happened to William Howard Taft . . . well, sort of.

On Christmas Eve 1920, he was meeting with the newly elected president Warren Harding who asked Taft if he would ever be interested in serving on the Supreme Court? It was an interesting question because being a justice on the nation's highest court had always been his dream job.

There are only nine justices on the Supreme Court so it is rare when a position is available. Also, a justice is always appointed by the president.

The next day, which happened to be Christmas, Taft wrote president-elect Harding a letter and told him that he would, "be very grateful for the honor" to have an opportunity to serve on the Supreme Court.

Former President Taft didn't have to wait very long to receive his wish. Six months after their meeting, there was an opening on the court at which time, he was chosen as the new justice by President Harding. He served there for the next nine years.

For William Howard Taft, President Harding would always be like Santa Claus because he made his ultimate wish come true.

Yes, it's true!

In 1915, a delivery man brings a load of Christmas trees to be sold in New York City using horses and a wagon (Library of Congress photo).

Chapter 25

Woodrow Wilson
The 28th President
Christmas Connections

Woodrow Wilson was the nation's twenty-eighth president. He was born three days after Christmas in 1856 which was the first of several connections that he had to the holiday season.

When he became president in 1913, among the first things that he wanted to do was to have a major Christmas celebration. It happened on Christmas Eve 1913, as more than 20,000 spectators gathered at the U.S. Capitol Building for the first national holiday festival in Washington, D.C. It was called, "A Civic Christmas."

The forty-five-minute program featured a chorus of 1,000 local singers along with the U.S. Marine Band and a costumed group who reenacted the Nativity of Christ. They entertained the gathering near a magnificent forty-foot Norway spruce Christmas tree with rows of red, white and blue electric bulbs and a brightly lit sign with the words, "Peace on earth, goodwill to men." The tree had been decorated by volunteers.

The ceremony was perfectly timed because the next day, it rained in Washington, D.C.

Two years later, one week before Christmas in 1915, President Wilson was busy as usual but he was attending to other matters than those of the country. It was on that day that he got married to Edith Galt at her home in Washington, D.C. It was a small wedding attended by their families and just a few friends.

The president loved his new wife but he also loved cars. He would often set aside time in his afternoon schedule to have the Secret Service drive him around Washington, D.C. On Christmas Day 1916, President Wilson and the First Lady loaded several automobiles with gifts and personally delivered them to poor children in the nation's capital. For the Commander-in-Chief, the caravan of vehicles acted as his personal sleigh and reindeer.

However, things changed in 1917 when American soldiers went off to Europe to fight in World War I. Because of that, there was no community Christmas tree lighting ceremony that year but the event resumed in 1918 after the war was over.

The president and First Lady were not in Washington, D.C., for the holiday season in 1918. World War I had ended in November which meant that he would have to travel to France to work out the terms of the peace treaty. This was in the days before long distance air travel took place so on December 4, President Wilson, his wife, and several staff members boarded the ship SS *George Washington* for the nine-day voyage. It was the first trip ever made to Europe by an American president.

On Christmas Day 1918, President Wilson spoke to 10,000 American soldiers who were stationed in France. Later that afternoon, he and the First Lady enjoyed Christmas dinner as the special guests at the headquarters of the U.S. top general John Pershing.

The president and his group returned home in February but made two more trips to France, by ship, in 1919. When he got back to the United States, President Wilson received a special gift. A new Pierce-Arrow, one of the most expensive cars of the day, had been added to the White House fleet. The nation's leader enjoyed the automobile so much that, two years later when he left office, his friends purchased it for him as a going away gift for his personal use. Today, the car is on display in the Woodrow Wilson Presidential Library Museum.

TODAY'S QUESTIONS

1. How tall was the Christmas Tree at "A Civic Christmas" celebration in 1913?
2. Why was there no community Christmas tree lighting ceremony in 1917?
3. Woodrow Wilson was the first president to visit Europe. How did he get there?

IT'S A FACT . . .

What if there were no toys under America's trees on Christmas morning? Believe it or not, it almost happened in 1917, when Woodrow Wilson was president, as the country was trying to conserve materials that could be used for the troops who were fighting in World War I. Among the items on that list were metal and cloth that were used to create weapons and supplies which meant that no toys would be made.

That's when A. C. Gilbert, a toy maker from Connecticut, began speaking out for the nation's children. He argued his case with government officials who finally agreed that there would be no ban on the manufacturing of toys, despite the war.

Soon after, newspapers began reporting the story which hailed Mr. Gilbert as the "Man Who Saved Christmas for the Children."

Yes, it's true!

President Harding shakes hands with Sally Lefevre while purchasing Christmas Seals at the White House (Library of Congress photo).

CHAPTER 26

Warren Harding
The 29th President
Helping Others at Christmas

Warren Harding's plan to become the nation's leader began during the holiday season a year before he was elected. On December 17, 1919, just a week before Christmas, the fifty-four-year-old Senator from Ohio announced that he would be running to become the country's twenty-ninth president.

One year later, after winning the nation's highest office, the newly elected president was busy making plans for his administration and moving into the White House. The Hardings's first Christmas in the mansion took place in 1921 and First Lady Florence was in charge of the season's decorations.

She originally planned to have lit candles placed in the window sills of all the rooms of the White House that faced Pennsylvania Avenue. That would allow the citizens who were walking past the famous structure to enjoy them. But Mrs. Harding was warned by the insurance industry that this could be dangerous by causing a fire hazard. Instead, she changed the plan and safely hung Christmas wreaths in the windows.

The First Lady also enjoyed visiting wounded soldiers of World War I who were residing at the Walter Reed Army Medical Center in Washington, D.C. As a gift to cheer them up, she would bring each of them a giant sized candy cane for Christmas. The recovering military men appreciated the First Lady's kindness.

A few weeks before Christmas 1922, Mrs. Harding became very ill with a kidney ailment and, even though she went through some difficult weeks, she recovered in time for the holidays. Before Christmas dinner that year, the president, who greatly enjoyed playing golf, got in an early round at one of his favorite courses in Maryland just a few miles from the White House.

The Hardings were enthusiastic supporters of the Christmas Seals campaign to fight the lung disease, tuberculosis. In the early twentieth century, it was the leading cause of death in the United States. A woman named Emily Bissell, whose cousin was a doctor, came up with an idea to raise money in order to fight the illness. She designed and printed special holiday stamps, known as seals, and sold them for a penny each. Emily's campaign was a huge success and Christmas Seals were created. The president participated in a fund-raising ad for Christmas Seals posing in a photograph with a child with tuberculosis (see the photo in this chapter).

Today, Christmas Seals are still available and are sold by the American Lung Association.

There was no television available for homes in the 1920s so radio was the major form of entertainment. On February 8, 1922, President Harding had the first radio installed in the White House. He then created history on June 14 by being the first president to be heard over the speakers of the popular sound box. That was followed on December 8, just two weeks before Christmas when President Harding became the first national leader to have his Annual Message to Congress broadcast over the radio.

In the summer of 1923, Warren Harding made his last trip as president. He traveled by train to Alaska, not far from Santa Claus and the North Pole.

TODAY'S QUESTIONS

1. What was Mrs. Harding going to put in the windows of the White House but was warned not to do so by the insurance industry?
2. What did Mrs. Harding give the wounded soldiers for a Christmas gift?
3. In 1922, President Harding put one of these in the White House. What was it?

IT'S A FACT . . .

For forty years, Horace Vose of Westerly, Rhode Island, was known as the "Poultry King." In 1873, he began a tradition of sending a turkey to the president every Christmas. That year, Mr. Vose shipped one of his big birds to President Ulysses S. Grant and his family for their holiday meal.

His turkeys were always thirty pounds or bigger. The custom continued until Mr. Vose died in 1913.

During the Christmas season of 1922, the Hardings received an unusual offering for their holiday meal from Gabe Burkhardt of Okmulgee, Oklahoma. He sent the First Family a live fifteen-pound white possum!

However, the possum was saved and replaced on the Christmas menu by a roast pig.

Yes, it's true!

A group of workers prepare the first National Christmas Tree for the ceremony in 1923 (Library of Congress photo).

Chapter 27

Calvin Coolidge
The 30th President

Let's Light the Tree!

Every year, one of the programs that millions of people look forward to watching on television is the annual White House Tree Lighting Ceremony. The highlight of this well-known activity features the president flipping a switch to turn on the lights to the National Christmas Tree. But how did it begin?

When Calvin Coolidge became president in 1923, there were those in Washington, D.C., who believed that the city needed to have a National Christmas Tree. The leader of that movement was Lucretia (pronounced Lou-cree-sha) Hardy, who worked with a group to improve Washington, D.C. In November of that year, she contacted the White House to propose her idea.

Her plan included having a large tree placed on the grounds of the White House followed by a celebration featuring singers and musicians. Soon afterward, the request was approved to move forward and Lucretia began working with the department in charge of public grounds in order to prepare for the festivities. However, since the tree lighting was scheduled for Christmas Eve, which was less than a month away, it meant that everyone who was involved needed to get busy.

The first task was to locate a very large Christmas tree that could be brought to Washington, D.C. The volunteers didn't have to wait very long to get what they wanted. Middlebury College was a small campus but it had several large and beautiful fir trees.

Dr. Paul Moody, the president of the school, offered to have one of them taken to Washington, D.C., for the ceremony. The gesture was almost too good to be true as Middlebury College happened to be located in President Coolidge's home state of Vermont.

Meanwhile, as several volunteers were working out the details of moving the tall timber to the nation's capital, another group was busy figuring out how it would be lit. It would take many electricians to do the job so that it was safe and properly working. On December 11, President Coolidge officially accepted the tree along with the plan for a lighting ceremony but time was running out as there were only two weeks remaining to pull everything together.

However, there was another problem. First Lady Grace Coolidge had already planned a caroling event for Christmas Eve on the White House lawn and did not want more than one holiday program at the mansion. She suggested having the tree lighting at an area known as the Ellipse located just south of the White House near the Washington Monument. The planners quickly made the decision to move the ceremony to the new location.

As the change of plans took place, a forty-eight-foot tall balsam fir tree at Middlebury College was cut down and loaded onto a special train car headed for Washington, D.C. It was so large that a few of the branches were broken during the journey but the tree arrived on December 14 and was taken to the Ellipse where it was erected. It was now time to decorate the huge timber.

The U.S. electrical industry donated $5,000 worth of electrical cables to help wire the area. Over the coming days, a total of 2,500 red, white, and green Christmas lights were added to the branches as other volunteers made sure that the events that had been scheduled would be ready to go. People across the nation were excited about the program because even though there was no television in those days, radio and newspapers had been reporting on the project from the beginning.

At 3:00 pm on Christmas Eve, a 100-voice choir from the First Congregational Church began a program of caroling on the White House grounds just as Mrs. Coolidge had planned. Two hours later, nearly 6,000 people watched as the president and his family walked from the mansion toward the Ellipse where the leader of the country pressed a button to light the first National Christmas Tree. Interestingly, electricity was still rather new to the American public and President Coolidge's small hometown of Plymouth Notch, Vermont, was one that still didn't have electric power.

The tree-lighting ceremony was followed by a forty-minute program of singing and bands playing Christmas favorites. To close out the evening, a lighted cross was displayed on the 555-foot-tall Washington monument. The first National Christmas Tree remained at the location for one year. The ceremony has become an American tradition which was televised for the first time in 1946.

Today's Questions

1. From what state was the first National Christmas Tree brought to Washington, D.C.?
2. What were the colors of the lights on the first National Christmas Tree?
3. Who lit the first National Christmas Tree?

It's a Fact . . .

Sometimes husbands forget things even if they are the president of the United States. During one Christmas, President Coolidge gave his wife twenty-five one-dollar gold coins as a gift but he forgot to include a card. Trying to cover his mistake, he presented one to her that had been given to him from a friend a few days earlier.

But the president's plan backfired because when the First Lady read the greeting, he had left the name of the person on the card who had originally sent it to him—his friend Frank Stearns! Sometimes, even the president gets it wrong.

Yes, it's true!

President Hoover inspects the damage to White House after the Christmas Eve fire of 1929 (Library of Congress photo).

Chapter 28

Herbert Hoover
The 31st President
The White House Is on Fire . . . Again!

Christmas Eve in 1929 started off the same as most others. At thirty-two degrees, it was a cold day in Washington, D.C., but the good news was that there was no rain or snow. For Herbert and Lou Hoover, it would be their first holiday season as the country's president and First Lady.

That year, Mrs. Hoover established a new tradition. For some time, the main White House Christmas tree was set up in the Blue Room. However, 1929 was the first where the wife of the president was in charge of decorating the tree. She chose a theme of men and horses made from gingerbread as the custom of the First Lady supervising the decorating continues today.

Mrs. Hoover made her way to the Central Union Mission where she passed out gifts to the city's disadvantaged children. At 6:00 pm, she and President Hoover took the short walk from the White House to Sherman Plaza for the annual lighting of the National Christmas Tree. Citizens from coast-to-coast were able to follow the event as it was broadcast by radio throughout the nation.

A few minutes later, the First Family returned to the White House where they were scheduled to host a party for young people and their parents. The Marine Band entertained the guests playing Christmas songs while refreshments were served, games played, and gifts were passed out to the visitors. It seemed that everyone in the main building was having a jolly old time.

But the White House is a very big place and the grounds take up a great deal of space in the nation's capital. There are other parts to the property in addition to the main house. The area where several of the offices are located, including the president's, is known as the West Wing. It was built in 1902 when Theodore Roosevelt was the nation's leader. However, that's where trouble struck on Christmas Eve 1929.

At 8:00 pm, as the party continued at the mansion, the switchboard operator M. M. Rice was in his office in the West Wing trying to keep busy. The job of a switchboard operator is to direct incoming telephone calls to the proper person. Being that it was Christmas Eve, there wasn't much to do that evening.

From his office, Mr. Rice began to smell smoke and immediately contacted the Secret Service. At that point, the fire department was called and shortly thereafter, fire trucks were on their way to America's most famous home. When they arrived, smoke could be seen billowing from several windows as the roof was already on fire. Since the sun had set, the temperature had dropped making it bitterly cold as the firefighters went to work.

While the fire grew in the West Wing, the gathering in the mansion continued and nobody noticed what was taking place outside. A member of the White House staff walked over to President Hoover and whispered, "The Executive Offices are on fire." The president and his son Allen, who was home for Christmas from college, along with several staff members excused themselves and left the festivities for the West Wing. Meanwhile, Mrs. Hoover remained with the children and guests and continued to keep the party going.

As firemen battled the blaze and smoke filled the rooms, the group went to the president's office and tried to remove as many of the files that they could. This was before there were computers so, in those days, files were made of paper that would burn quickly unless they could be saved. The Secret Service soon arrived at the office and removed President Hoover and the others to a safe area.

This wasn't the first time that the White House was burned as its most famous fire took place on August 24, 1814, during the War of 1812, when British troops entered Washington, D.C., and torched the building which did a great amount of damage to America's mansion.

The fire was getting worse as wires were burned cutting off the electricity. There was also no fresh air in the stairways which made it difficult for the firefighters. However, there was another problem; two fire engines arrived but couldn't enter the grounds because the massive iron gates were locked and barred. The Secret Service had recently changed the locks but failed to notify the Fire Department. That forced the firefighters to wait for several minutes in the cold weather with a portion of the White House burning until a police officer could get the keys to open the gates.

As the fire grew, so did the number of spectators who gathered on the street. About 150 soldiers along with 100 police officers were called in to form a human wall to hold back the crowds. They watched as the flames lit up the night's sky.

After about two hours, the firefighters were able to get the blaze under control. By then, many of the party guests had arrived home and learned about the fire for the first time when they turned on their radios. As the evening continued, they had no idea what had taken place at the West Wing. Mrs. Hoover had been able to keep her guests safe and calm.

Fifteen firemen were injured doing their duty in fighting the blaze, but the good news was that no lives were lost. An investigation followed where it was discovered that the cause of the fire was found to be an overheated flue in one of the White House's many fireplaces. A flue is an opening in a chimney that releases gases from a fireplace to the outdoors.

Over the next year (1930) several offices along with the roof on the West Wing had to be remodeled and replaced. The Secret Service also made sure that the Fire Chief was given a set of keys to the White House gates that worked.

Today's Questions

1. Where were the Hoovers when the fire broke out?
2. In what area of the White House did the fire take place?
3. Why couldn't the two fire trucks get to the White House?

It's a Fact . . .

In 1930, when the West Wing of the White House was being repaired from the fire damage, it produced a large amount of scrap wood. The Hoovers had some of the pieces from the historic event made into Christmas gifts for their staff members. They included bookends and other small items. Each gift had an engraved card with a poem written by Mrs. Hoover. The guests who had been at the White House a year earlier when the fire broke out were given a toy fire truck from the president.

Yes, it's true!

President Roosevelt holding two of his grandchildren during Christmas 1939 (FDR Library photo).

Chapter 29

Franklin D. Roosevelt
The 32nd President
The 12 Years of Christmas

Franklin D. Roosevelt served three complete terms in office and was elected to a fourth which meant that he spent more years as president than anyone else. It also meant that he was the nation's leader for twelve straight Christmas holidays; however, not everyone in the United States was enjoying themselves.

During that era, two events created difficult times for Americans. The first was the Great Depression which lasted for several years. It was a period when many businesses failed and people were without work which meant that they had nothing for Christmas. A large number of children became orphans because their families had no money to support them.

The other major event was World War II, which saw the United States fighting in two areas of the world, Europe and the South Pacific. It caused many soldiers to be away from their families during the Christmas holidays while they were defending the country. All in all, it was a tough time to be the leader of the country.

Christmas was special to the Roosevelts. The president had been born and raised in Hyde Park, New York, where he was a sort of Christmas tree farmer. Each year, he planted young evergreens on his home grounds when they were just six inches high. Over time, he would tend to them and then have them cut down and sell them after ten years of growth. Local tree dealers would always scurry to buy up the Roosevelt trees.

Franklin and Eleanor Roosevelt moved into the White House in March 1933. As the new president went to work on helping those who had been affected by the Great Depression, the First Lady went Christmas shopping. The Roosevelts had a large family that included five children, their spouses, and thirteen grandchildren which meant that it would take time to get everyone the right gift.

On the third floor of the White House, Mrs. Roosevelt hid her family's presents in a special small room known as the "Christmas Closet." She would buy so many gifts that she wrote them on a list in order to keep track of all of them.

Franklin wasn't the first Roosevelt to become president. His cousin, Theodore, had held the office some thirty years earlier. As a young man, he was stricken with the disease polio which confined him to a wheelchair for the remainder of his life. At times, this made it difficult for him to travel to places so Mrs. Roosevelt would often attend in his place. A cure for polio was discovered in the 1950s by Dr. Jonas Salk and today the vaccine is one of the shots given to babies shortly after they are born.

Like other First Ladies, Eleanor Roosevelt would visit local charities on Christmas Eve before hosting an event at the White House. In the evening, the First Family would light the National Christmas Tree and then gather in the mansion's East Room with their grandchildren and friends as President Roosevelt read "The Night before Christmas" to them.

Following a busy day that included many events, Mrs. Roosevelt would leave the White House for a while to attend a midnight service at her church. That year (1933), the First Family received more than 300,000 Christmas Cards with best wishes from citizens throughout the country.

Although when it came to giving gifts, the couple each had different ideas of how it should be done. Mrs. Roosevelt liked to give people different types of gifts while the president believed in one for all. In 1934, Mr. Roosevelt presented each member of his staff an autographed copy of his book, *On Our Way*, which explained his ideas on how to rescue the country from the Great Depression.

By 1940, much of Europe was at war. That year, Mrs. Roosevelt wrote a children's book titled *Christmas: A Story*. It was the tale of a little Dutch girl named Martha whose father is killed in the war. It wasn't her last work as she wrote another Christmas book that was released in 1962.

Christmas 1941 was difficult for the United States because it had just entered World War II a few days earlier. That year, the Roosevelts hosted a special guest for Christmas when British Prime Minister Winston Churchill spent the holidays at the White House. His country was also at war but were fighting on the same side with the United States. He and the president spent many hours laying out plans to defeat the enemy nations as the rest of the Roosevelt family held their regular holiday celebration.

On Christmas Eve, Prime Minister Churchill joined the Roosevelts for the lighting of the National Christmas Tree. No doubt the guest felt comfortable in the United States because although he was the Prime Minister of Great Britain, Mr. Churchill's mother was an American. The ceremony that year drew a crowd of more than 20,000 spectators but, due to the war, it was the last tree lighting by a president until 1945.

The Roosevelts spent the Christmas seasons of 1943 and 1944 away from Washington, D.C. They returned to New York and enjoyed a family gathering at their home at Hyde Park. By then, the president had been adding to his private collection of Christmas cards for several years. It included more than 3,000 different designs.

By 1945, President Roosevelt had fallen into ill health and died in April. But the work that he had done with Prime Minister Churchill paid off a few weeks later as the enemy nations surrendered and World War II was over. It meant that a large number of the soldiers would return to the United States and be home in time for Christmas.

Today's Questions

1. What did Franklin Roosevelt grow on his property in Hyde Park, New York?
2. Every Christmas Eve, Franklin Roosevelt read a story to a group of children. What was that story?
3. Why weren't the lights on the National Christmas Tree lit after 1941?

It's a Fact . . .

Black Friday is not an official holiday, but it has become one of those days of the year that many people look forward to participating. It has become famous as the day after Thanksgiving where many stores hold huge sales of their products meaning bargain prices for their customers. But how did this begin?

In 1939, President Roosevelt declared that he was moving Thanksgiving Day up a week, to the second-to-last Thursday in the month. The reason was to allow citizens an extra week to do their Christmas shopping which would help the store owners who were suffering through the Great Depression. But the plan didn't work and two years later, Thanksgiving returned to its original position on the last Thursday of the month.

However, stores across the country began having day after Thanksgiving sales which drew huge crowds of customers. In the 1960s, police in the city of Philadelphia complained because there were so many shoppers that they clogged the streets and sidewalks and so officers began calling it, "Black Friday."

Yes, it's true!

In 1950, busy workers continued to renovate the White House (Truman Library photo).

Chapter 30

Harry S. Truman
The 33rd President
Christmas in Independence

Everything gets old. People, pets, cars, even houses. Especially houses, because no matter how big or how small, over time they all need work. Sometimes it's just minor repairs but on other occasions, it may require a major renovation.

Some of the most famous houses in history have needed a great deal of work. One of those is the most well-known home in the United States, the White House. When a mansion is nearly 150 years old with so many rooms and offices to care for, it means that at some point, there is going to have to be repairs. Even with a full-time staff who were in charge of its upkeep, the massive structure was in need of work.

The person who would have to make the decisions on repairing the White House was Harry Truman. In 1945, he had become the nation's thirty-third president but when he moved into the executive mansion, it was already showing signs of wear and tear. The famous building had been the site of two fires, many rough winters, thousands of visitors, and other happenings that were causing it to show its age.

Repairs to the structure were not at the top of the president's "to-do" list when he took office. There were other important matters that took up his time such as drawing an end to World War II, working out a peace treaty, and bringing the soldiers home. But by Christmas 1945 almost all of those things had been taken care of and the nation was a happy place once again. In fact, for the first time in four years, the National Christmas Tree was lit by the president on Christmas Eve.

A crowd of 10,000 turned out to watch Harry Truman light the tree for his first time as president. He then told the crowd, "This is the Christmas that a war-weary world has prayed for through long and awful years. With peace comes joy and gladness. The gloom of the war years fades as once more we light the National Community Christmas Tree."

Once those matters had been addressed, President Truman could turn his attention to other things—like the problems in the White House. By 1947, the situation was getting scary. It wasn't unusual to feel the second story floor moving or seeing the grand chandelier swaying back and forth. The problem got so bad that the presidential bathtub began sinking into the floor and a leg from a piano broke through the surface of another room.

Things got even worse the following year when President Truman said, "I've had the second floor where we live examined—and it is about to fall down! I'm having it shored up and hoping to have a concrete and steel floor put in before I leave here."

For the country, 1948 was an election year which meant that the Truman Family spent election night, and several more days after that, in their hometown of Independence, Missouri. Even though the president had won the election, there was a surprise waiting for Trumans when they returned to the White House. The official engineer and architect would not allow them into the mansion!

The president told his sister, "Found the White House in one terrible shape. . . . We've had to call off all functions and will move out as soon as I come back from Key West (Florida)."

However, that wasn't the last of the bad news. When the First Family returned two weeks later from their vacation to Key West, the people in charge of the repairs told them that nothing could be saved but the outside walls. The entire inside of the house would have to be gutted and rebuilt. A major part of the job required all of the wooden beams that had been used to build the White House in the 1790s would need to be replaced with steel and concrete. This had to be done to hold up the extreme weight of the building.

They had originally believed that the job would take a few months but it was now estimated that it would take several years.

It was one month before Christmas and the First Family had just been told that they would have to move out of the White House. When they did, the Trumans didn't go far. In fact, they went across the street to Blair House which is a residence that is used when important visitors would come to Washington, D.C., to meet with the president.

As the holidays approached, having a Christmas gathering was not a problem because, at that point, the Trumans had spent every season except one in their hometown of Independence, Missouri. The president preferred to be in the area where he had grown up and away from the politicians in Washington, D.C. He summed up his feelings one year in a speech that he gave over the radio when he said, "For of all the days of the year, Christmas is the family day."

The Trumans didn't have a large amount of money like many other presidential families but they were close to each other. They lived in an average house on a regular street which is just the way that the president liked it. By 1948, he and his wife had owned their home for twenty-nine years.

The Trumans spent the Christmases of 1949, 1950, and 1951 with family members in Independence. In March 1952, the final repairs to the White House were finished and they were able to return after living at Blair House for almost four years. At about that time, the president decided not to run for reelection but did choose to spend his final holiday season as the nation's leader at the White House. With its renovations completed, the First Couple gave to each member of their staff a photograph of the newly repaired White House that included a gold Presidential Seal along with the words, "Christmas Greetings from the President and Mrs. Truman, 1952."

On January 20, 1953, Dwight D. Eisenhower replaced Harry Truman as president and, after almost eight years in office, he returned home to Independence as a private citizen. Over the years, he continued to celebrate the holidays with family members in his hometown where he would often greet visitors at his presidential library and museum. In 1972, the eighty-eight-year-old former president passed away . . . on the day after Christmas.

TODAY'S QUESTIONS

1. Why were the Trumans told that they would have to move out of the White House?
2. Where is Blair House?
3. Where did the Trumans spend most of their Christmas holidays?

IT'S A FACT . . .

The number one song during Christmas week 1949, when Harry Truman was president, was "Rudolph the Red-Nosed Reindeer" sung by country-western star Gene Autry. The recording sold 2 1/2 million copies the first year and, since then, has sold more than 25 million.

Yes, it's true!

Dwight Eisenhower's painting of Abraham Lincoln that was used on the 1953 official presidential Christmas cards (Dwight D. Eisenhower Library and Museum).

Chapter 31

Dwight D. Eisenhower
The 34th President
The Painting President

President Dwight D. Eisenhower was a unique person. After serving forty-one years in the military, he was twice elected president of the United States. He also enjoyed art, cooking, writing, and playing golf.

Eisenhower graduated from the United States Military Academy at West Point, New York; rose to the rank of general; and was one of the heroes of World War II.

During his years in the army, he and his wife Mamie moved many times. In fact, the Eisenhowers relocated so often, that they didn't own a home until 1950 when they bought an old farm in Gettysburg, Pennsylvania. By then General Eisenhower was sixty years old.

In 1952, he ran for president and won. It was just like another famous general who became the nation's leader, Ulysses S. Grant, who was also elected the first time that he ever ran for office.

In 1953, the Eisenhowers spent their first Christmas in the White House. That year, history was made as the first Christmas card was created by a U.S. president. He enjoyed painting and did a portrait of Abraham Lincoln. When it was finished, the Hallmark Company produced more than a thousand cards displaying the president's artwork. They were given to government officials and staff members at the mansion. Those that remain today are considered to be collector's items and are very valuable.

That holiday season was also the first time that President Eisenhower lit the National Community Christmas Tree as more than 4,000 spectators watched. His speech that followed was broadcast around the world by radio in more than thirty different languages. With the popularity of his

Christmas cards, the following year the president repeated the gesture and painted a portrait of George Washington that was used on them.

Mrs. Eisenhower enjoyed the holidays and decorating the White House for Christmas which included having garland wrapped around its massive outdoor columns. There were bright red bows throughout and mistletoe hung from the crystal chandeliers. She also had the windows sprayed with a white powder that resembled snowflakes.

The staff lovingly referred to the First Lady as "Mrs. Christmas." She often received letters from parents who were too poor to buy Christmas gifts for their children. She would then take many of the gifts that were sent to her grandchildren from citizens around the country and donate them to charity so that those who had little would receive a gift for the holiday.

Each year, the Eisenhowers threw a Christmas party for the White House staff. This was not a small get-together as the crowd usually reached around 500 people. Mrs. Eisenhower would purchase gifts for all and then wrap them herself in order to save money.

For their first two Christmases as the First Family, the Eisenhowers didn't stay in the nation's capital. They traveled to Augusta, Georgia, where the president owned a cabin located at his favorite golf course. He enjoyed the game so much that he played every Wednesday afternoon and Saturday mornings at a private course near Washington, D.C. He even had an area where he would practice just outside of his office at the White House.

Christmas 1958 at the mansion was bigger than ever. It featured twenty-seven decorated trees including one that was done in the First Lady's favorite color—pink. Christmas music was piped into every room and, once again, President Eisenhower made history when his Christmas address was broadcast by satellite. The United States had launched its first ever space satellite in January 1958 and today, most radio and television stations use these spacecraft to transmit their programs.

President Eisenhower's final year in office was 1960 and he went out in a big way. For the National Christmas Tree that year, he chose a Douglas fir from Oregon that was seventy-five feet tall. It was the second time that a tree so big was chosen for the ceremony during the Eisenhower presidency and, at that time, was the tallest ever chosen for the event.

Today's Questions

1. What did Dwight D. Eisenhower do for forty-one years before he became president?
2. What was President Eisenhower's favorite sport?

3. What type of space object was used to broadcast President Eisenhower's Christmas Address of 1958?

IT'S A FACT . . .

In October 1957, while Dwight D. Eisenhower was president, the well-known book *The Grinch Who Stole Christmas* by Dr. Seuss was released. A few years later, it was made into a television program and then a movie.
   Yes, it's true!

The President and Mrs. Kennedy take a look at one of the many White House Christmas trees in 1961 (public doman photo by Robert Knudsen).

Chapter 32

John F. Kennedy
The 35th President
The Christmas Theme

On January 20, 1961, John F. Kennedy was sworn in as the nation's thirty-fifth president. At the age of forty-three, he also became the youngest person ever elected to the nation's highest office.

It meant that for the first time in many years, the country would have a young family living in the White House. When the Kennedys moved into the mansion following the inauguration ceremony, their daughter Caroline was only three-and-a-half years old and their son John, Jr. was two months. In fact, he was born just two weeks after his dad's election.

The Kennedys were different than many of the First Families that had recently lived in the White House. Those that had come before them like the Roosevelts, Trumans, and Eisenhowers also had children but they were adults. For most, their families included grandchildren as had other past presidents. But the new First Family was different in a number of ways than many of the others.

Having little children around wasn't the only change that the Kennedys brought to the mansion. Chapter 30 told the story of how the White House had to be rebuilt on the inside during the Truman presidency after many years of wear. Much of the old wood frame, plumbing, and other parts of the construction had to be modernized. However, there was still another area that needed attention.

Many of the items around the historic home were also in poor shape. It was time for some of the furniture and other pieces to be replaced. In April 1961, Mrs. Kennedy set about to restore the inside of the White House. She wanted to display some of the antiques that had been in storage which would give the residence more of the look of a museum and show off its history.

When December arrived, workers continued upgrading the mansion as Mrs. Kennedy prepared it for Christmas. That year, she became the first First Lady to decorate the residence using a common theme. For 1961, she chose the characters from the famous ballet, the *Nutcracker Suite*. The idea was so popular that since then, every First Lady has chosen a Christmas theme for the White House.

Have you ever watched the *Nutcracker Suite*?

Christmas activities in the nation's capital kept Mrs. Kennedy busy as she sponsored a party for disadvantaged local children and visited a home for youngsters who had been abandoned or orphaned. She also visited the Children's Hospital handing out presents to those who were hospitalized during the holidays.

After slightly more than a year, the job of restoring the inside of the mansion was complete. On February 14, 1962, citizens in the United States and many other countries got a chance to see all of the improvements as Mrs. Kennedy hosted a one-hour television special. She took camera crews on a guided tour of the $2 million in upgrades. The program was watched by 80 million viewers, not only in the United States, but also in fifty other countries around the world including Russia and China.

As Christmas 1962 approached, Mrs. Kennedy traveled to New York City, where she had grown up, to do some holiday shopping. Since her husband's election, she had become a national celebrity and was very popular. At one store, the mob of people trying to approach her to get an autograph or shake her hand was so large that she quickly had to be taken back to her hotel by the Secret Service. She later said, "It seems I can't go anywhere anymore without causing a scene."

Like several other presidential families had done, the Kennedys spent Christmas away from the White House. The president came from a large and wealthy family that would gather at Palm Beach, Florida, for the holidays. His parents owned a big home that faced the ocean with its own beach which is where they celebrated Christmas in 1961 and 1962.

After her first Christmas in Palm Beach as First Lady, Mrs. Kennedy noticed that the Secret Service agents who traveled with her family to Florida had to spend their holidays without their loved ones. She had become friends with several of the bodyguards and the following year, she made sure that their wives also traveled with the Kennedys for Christmas.

Perhaps the happiest person in America to see 1962 draw to an end was President Kennedy. It had been a very difficult year which nearly saw the United States and their bitter enemy, the Soviet Union (Russia), almost go to war. But the two countries were able to settle their differences which meant that they could each focus on other important matters.

On the week before Thanksgiving 1963, the president and First Lady departed on a three-day trip to Texas. He had decided to run for reelection the following year and believed that it would be a good time to do some early campaigning. Shortly before the Kennedys left on their journey, they received their official Christmas cards from Hallmark for that year and signed thirty of them. The card's message read, "With our wishes for a Blessed Christmas and a Happy New Year."

They planned to sign the rest when they returned to the White House. But that would never happen because President Kennedy died during his trip. Although, the cards were never mailed, a few still exist today and are quite valuable. They are the rarest of any presidential Christmas cards and several have been sold for thousands of dollars.

That year, due to President Kennedy's death, the National Christmas Tree was not lit until December 22nd following a national thirty-day period of mourning. At the ceremony, the new president, Lyndon Johnson said in his Christmas address, "Today we come to the end of a season of great national sorrow, and to the beginning of the season of great, eternal joy. We mourn our great President, John F. Kennedy, but he would have us go on."

During her time as First Lady, Mrs. Kennedy designed three different Christmas cards. Two of them, the Gift of the Magi and Good Tidings were printed and then sold to the general public in a limited edition. The money from those card sales was used to help build the John F. Kennedy Center for the Performing Arts in Washington, D.C.

Today's Questions

1. What was the first theme used by Mrs. Kennedy for a White House Christmas?
2. What happened when Mrs. Kennedy tried to go Christmas shopping in New York City?
3. In 1963, the president and Mrs. Kennedy signed thirty of these before they left for Texas. What were they?

It's a Fact . . .

One of the most popular television programs on the air while John F. Kennedy was president was the animated series *The Flintstones*. The toys that were produced which were based off of the show's characters were among the most asked for Christmas gifts of the early 1960s.

Yes, it's true!

President Johnson on Christmas Eve 1968 with his family at the White House (Photo by Frank Wolfe).

Chapter 33

Lyndon B. Johnson
The 36th President
A Texas-Sized Christmas

Lyndon Johnson became the thirty-sixth president of the United States in November 1963. There was no doubt that anybody would ever mistake him for Santa Claus. He was a tall, tough-talking Texan who had spent many years in politics and had wanted to be president for a long time.

However, the 1960s were a challenging era that made being the leader of the country more difficult than one might expect. To escape the many problems, there were the winter holidays which gave the First Family an opportunity to go home to their beloved Texas ranch. Just one month after President Kennedy's death, the Johnsons were back on their 2,700-acre spread near the town of Stonewall among 400 head of Hereford cattle.

It was a place where President Johnson could relax while deer hunting or riding horses. Unfortunately, he couldn't get away from his biggest problem—the Vietnam War. U.S. troops had been fighting in that region of Southeast Asia for several years and, as time passed, more American soldiers were being sent there. While the rest of his family enjoyed the holidays, President Johnson kept busy on the telephone and in meetings as he directed the war from his ranch.

Time passed and as Christmas 1964 approached, some changes were being made at the mansion. Hallmark had produced the official White House Christmas cards since the Eisenhower presidency but that year, the American Greetings Corporation of Cleveland, Ohio, replaced them. For their first card, the company featured the Johnsons's daughters, Lynda and Luci, playing with the First Family's two pet beagles, Him and Her. In all, more than 30,000 cards were produced for the Johnsons that year.

Going back to his days as a senator and then vice president, Lyndon Johnson had always been a big supporter of the space program. Among other things, he wanted the United States to be the first country to put a human being on the moon. Little did he know that a couple of astronauts had planned a practical joke from space for the holiday season of 1965.

American astronauts Wally Schirra (pronounced Sure-rah) and Tom Stafford had completed their journey and were headed back to Earth aboard their spacecraft Gemini 6. On December 16, the pair radioed Mission Control to report that they had seen a U.F.O. (Unidentified Flying Object). They told the ground crew in Houston, we have an object, looks like a satellite going from north to south, probably in polar orbit. . . . Looks like he might be going to re-enter soon. . . . You just might let me pick up that thing. . . . I see a command module and eight smaller modules in front. The pilot of the command module is wearing a red suit.

As the curious engineers back at Mission Control checked their computers to find out what was happening, Commander Schirra coolly pulled out his harmonica and began playing "Jingle Bells." After the song, one of the controllers radioed the astronauts and told them about their space joke, "You're too much." A short while later, the crew landed safely back on Earth.

Although there were beautiful cards, wonderful gifts, and magnificent Christmas trees throughout the White House, the war in Vietnam lingered on. But in 1966, there seemed to be a glimmer of hope that peace may be on its way. The two sides, the United States and the North Vietnamese, agreed on a forty-eight-hour Christmas truce.

A truce is an agreement between the sides that are at war to temporarily cease fighting. In this case, it meant that they would stop on December 24 and 25. Many in the United States who wanted the battles to end saw the truce as a possible breakthrough but it wasn't so as once the deadline passed, the fighting began again.

On December 19, 1967, as most of the public was preparing for Christmas, President Johnson left on a world tour that took him to six different countries in just four-and-a-half days. His third stop was to Vietnam where he spoke with his generals, visited wounded soldiers, and awarded medals to many of them for their bravery. He finished the tour and by Christmas Day, the president was back at the ranch.

Christmas 1968 was the Johnsons's last as the nation's First Family but it wasn't the happiest of times. They decided to remain in Washington, D.C., over the holidays since they only had a few weeks left in the White House. President Johnson chose not to run for reelection which meant that he would soon be replaced. Between managing the war and the nation's other problems, he felt that his time as the country's leader had come to an end.

While the Johnsons celebrated Christmas, there were two important people who were missing from their family. Their daughters' husbands were in the military and both were serving in Vietnam. Each of them returned home safely but the war did not end until 1975.

When Lyndon Johnson left office in 1969, he had been the president for just a little more than five years. It had been a difficult time but when it was over, he said good-bye to the White House and went back to the place that he loved where he would spend the rest of his life doing the things that he enjoyed including celebrating Christmas—at his ranch in Texas.

President Johnson was always seen by the public as a man with well-trimmed hair who wore nice business suits. But on Christmas Eve 1971, he changed that look as he donned a well-known red suit and false beard. He then took a seat atop his tractor, and made the short drive to the hangar at his ranch's private airstrip. Awaiting him inside were the families of his employees.

It became a tradition for them to receive their gifts from the former president dressed as Santa Claus who also carried a bag of toys for the occasion.

For those people, the Johnson Ranch became the Texas version of the North Pole.

TODAY'S QUESTIONS

1. In what state was President Johnson's ranch?
2. What was the song that astronaut Wally Schirra played on his harmonica from space?
3. The husbands of President Johnson's daughters were not with the family when they celebrated Christmas in 1968. Where were they?

IT'S A FACT . . .

On December 21, 1968, President Johnson wrote a good luck message to the crew of Apollo 8 as they began a six-day mission that would see them become the first people to orbit the moon. Three days later on Christmas Eve, the largest television audience in history estimated at 1 billion people around the world, watched as they saw something never witnessed before by the human eye—the planet Earth!

From inside the Apollo 8 spacecraft, astronauts Frank Borman, Jim Lovell, and Bill Anders pointed a small television camera toward Earth that was transmitted to the viewers. Although the television picture wasn't perfect, those who saw it realized that they were watching an important historical event. The crew then took the famous photograph of the Earth that has been seen by many across the world since then.

They then read from the Book of Genesis in the King James Version of the *Bible*. The astronauts each took a turn reciting from verses 1 through 10. Commander Borman then concluded the broadcast as he told the audience, "And from the crew of Apollo 8, we close with good night, good luck, a Merry Christmas—and God bless all of you, all of you on the good Earth."

Seven months later, in July 1969, for the first time ever, man walked on the moon.

Yes, it is true!

Chapter 34

Richard Nixon
The 37th President
New Traditions

When Richard Nixon was elected the nation's thirty-seventh president in November 1968, he already knew a few things about the job. That's because for eight years (1953–1961), he had served as vice president under Dwight Eisenhower. He also knew what it was like to come up short as he did when he lost a close election for the White House in 1960 to John F. Kennedy.

As Mr. Nixon settled into his new position as the nation's leader, there was one important matter that hadn't been taken care of by President Johnson before he left office. It was the Vietnam War. He had not been able to bring about a lasting peace before the end of his term and it would now be up to the new president to try to stop the fighting in Southeast Asia.

While President Nixon dealt with the war, his wife Pat along with daughters Julie and Tricia, took over the job of decorating the White House when the holiday season approached. The First Lady had a keen sense of history and displayed many items from past Christmases at the mansion for others to see.

She had wreaths hung on the outside windows just as Mrs. Harding had done in the 1920s. There were glass cases set along the wall that held a number of items such as three Christmas cards from the 1870s that were received by President Rutherford B. Hayes along with the dollhouse that he had made by the White House carpenters for his daughter Frances.

It was also during Christmas 1969 that the first gingerbread house became part of the White House holiday decorations. The tasty creation is prepared by the mansion's kitchen staff and is always a main feature that gets bigger each year with additional pieces of candy, gingerbread men, and other fun items added to the newest version.

Also for their first White House Christmas, the Nixons began another tradition of giving presidential portraits to their staff members as gifts. For 1969, each staffer was presented a copy of the famous painting of George Washington by Gilbert Stuart. In addition, the First Family sent out 37,000 Christmas cards.

In 1970, Mrs. Nixon continued to introduce new programs like her "Candlelight Tours." She wanted to share the White House decorations with as many people as possible so the mansion was opened to the public for evening visitors. With the Christmas lights turned on and the Marine Band playing holiday music, the tours were a big success. One such group that took part was made up of sixty blind students from Los Angeles, who the First Lady guided through the mansion, describing the decorated areas to them.

President Nixon had played the piano since he was a boy growing up in California. He would often play "Rudolph the Red-Nosed Reindeer" for visiting friends and family members during the holidays. The president also had the exterior of the White House lighted so that those traveling along Pennsylvania Avenue could see the mansion at night for the first time. The gift for staff members that year was a copy of a portrait of Thomas Jefferson.

Away from Washington, D.C., the Nixons owned two homes, one in California and the other in Florida. Each sat near the ocean and had their own beaches. Whenever he could, the president and his family would try to take a few days during the holiday season to relax in Florida.

On Christmas morning 1971, President Nixon made a telephone call to a person who had once held his job. He spoke with former president Lyndon Johnson, whom he had known for many years, who was retired and living at his ranch in Texas. It is not unusual for a president to call another but it is usually to discuss the nation's business. In this case, Mr. Nixon simply wanted to wish Mr. Johnson a "Merry Christmas."

The year of 1972 was a busy one for Richard Nixon. He ran for reelection and won a second term and also became the first American president to visit the countries of China and the Soviet Union (Russia). He wanted to end the war in Vietnam and launched a major attack against the enemy during the Christmas holidays but the plan didn't succeed and the fighting continued into 1973. His Christmas gift to his staff members was a portrait of former president Theodore Roosevelt.

The final White House Christmas for the Nixons was 1973. In honor of the soldiers in Vietnam, only the top and four outer lights of the National Community Christmas Tree were turned on at the ceremony. Mrs. Nixon also cut back on the use of Christmas lights inside the mansion due to the energy crisis.

One of main reasons for the concerns about energy was that shortly before Christmas, the price of oil quadrupled making it four times more expensive than before. By the time that the holidays rolled around, many families who usually traveled during Christmas were forced to stay home. High prices on gasoline kept many of them off of the roads.

That year marked the fiftieth anniversary of the National Community Christmas Tree lighting ceremony. During the presentation, President Nixon lit the tall timber along with the help of a Boy Scout and a Girl Scout. In another change to save energy, a large number of lights on the tree were replaced by decorations and garland.

The First Family ordered 60,000 Christmas cards for 1973. That was almost twice as many as they had prepared for their first White House Christmas. In August 1974, the Nixons left the White House for the last time and returned to their home in California.

The First Lady and President Nixon join a friend on the White House lawn (Richard Nixon Foundation photo).

TODAY'S QUESTIONS

1. The Nixons's first Christmas at the mansion featured a house as one of the decorations. What kind of food was used to make it?
2. Why did Mrs. Nixon want to have "Candlelight Tours" of the White House?
3. What song did President Nixon enjoy playing on the piano?

IT'S A FACT . . .

Richard Nixon won the presidential election in November 1968 but there was something that he needed to take care of before assuming office on January 20. It was his daughter Julie's wedding.

Everything took place as planned and she got married three days before Christmas in New York City.

Her new husband was David Eisenhower, the grandson of President Dwight D. Eisenhower. Julie had known him since she was nine years old because her father had been the vice president under President Eisenhower.

Yes, it's true!

CHAPTER 35

Gerald Ford
The 38th President
Christmas on the Slopes

When the Christmas holidays arrive, it's not unusual to see a number of Americans enjoying ski trips. For those who live in the east, the mountains of Vermont are a popular place to glide over the snow. Meanwhile, for western residents, the Rocky Mountains of Colorado have always been a favorite location for skiers.

Vail is a small town in the western part of the state. Only about 5,000 persons actually live there full time but the population grows during the winter months as skiers roll in to take advantage of the fresh snow that covers the surrounding peaks. Many famous people such as entertainers and professional athletes can often be seen enjoying the beautiful area.

However, in the 1970s, one of the most recognized people in the world spent his Christmases in the small town. President Gerald Ford enjoyed snow skiing. In fact, he liked many different sports. That is because when he was in college, he was an outstanding athlete. Following his last year at the University of Michigan, Mr. Ford was offered a contract to play professional football but turned it down in order to attend law school.

He became vice president in 1973 and took over as president the next year. Like many of the nation's leaders, he wanted to get away from Washington, D.C., for the holidays. Others, such as Richard Nixon, enjoyed the warm beaches of Florida during their winter vacation.

But President Ford liked skiing and Vail offered some of the best slopes in the United States. So for his three years as president (1974–1975 and 1976), the First Family spent Christmas in Colorado. In 1939, the president learned to ski while living in New England. In 1968, he vacationed in Colorado for the first time and enjoyed it so much that he later built a second home there. Over the years, he did a great deal to help the sport and in 2001, he was elected to the Colorado Ski and Snowboard Hall of Fame.

However, there was more to Christmas with the Fords than just skiing. During their time in the White House, Mrs. Ford used handmade crafts to decorate some of the mansion's trees. The ornaments were made by residents from the Appalachian Mountains. The First Lady encouraged Americans everywhere to make their own decorations in order to save money and energy and also offered a White House booklet on how to put together homemade Christmas tree ornaments.

On December 17, 1974, President Ford lit the National Community Christmas Tree for the first time. That year's tall timber was a living forty-two-foot Colorado blue spruce from Pennsylvania.

The year of 1975 was special for the United States because it brought an end to the war in Vietnam. It meant that many families would be reunited with loved ones who had been away serving their country in the military.

With the end of the war, the Fords wanted to do something special for Christmas in 1975 to help kick off the celebration of America's 200th birthday the following year. For the patriotic theme, the National Christmas Tree was decorated with 4,600 red, white, and blue ornaments and 12,000 lights. There was also a replica of the Liberty Bell as part of its decorations. In addition, there were thirteen smaller trees representing the thirteen colonies and forty-four other trees placed in a row to honor the remaining states and territories.

For their final White House Christmas in 1976, the Fords ordered 25,000 Presidential Christmas cards. Each had a print of the painting, "Going to Church" by the famous artist George Henry Durrie, which displayed a white New England church with a pointed steeple in a winter setting as the townspeople make their way to the door.

After the Fords left the White House for the last time in January 1977, they divided their time between their two homes. During the warm months they lived in California where the former president enjoyed playing golf. However, as winter approached and the snow began to fall in Colorado, they packed up their equipment and enjoyed many weeks of skiing and some great memories of Christmas past.

TODAY'S QUESTIONS

1. What sport offered President Ford the chance to be a professional athlete?
2. Where did the Ford family spend their Christmas holidays?
3. In 1976, the United States celebrated a birthday. How old was the country?

President Gerald Ford takes some time to enjoy one of his favorite activities—skiing (Gerald R. Ford Library and Museum photo).

IT'S A FACT . . .

President Ford was no stranger to Christmas trees as in the summer of 1936, he worked as a ranger at Yellowstone National Park which has miles of forest where the tall timber grows wild. He later recalled that time as, "One of the greatest summers of my life."

Yes, it's true!

First Daughter Amy Carter admires the gingerbread house prepared by the White House chef in 1977 (Jimmy Carter Presidential Library and Museum photo).

Chapter 36

Jimmy Carter
The 39th President
A Small-Town Christmas

Jimmy Carter was sworn into office as the nation's thirty-ninth president on January 20, 1977. Just like the other leaders of the nation, he received all of the rewards of the world's most powerful job like living in the White House, flying about on the jumbo jet Air Force One, riding in limousines, and having a full staff of people to take care of him and his family.

When the holiday season arrived in December, it was more of the same. President Carter lit the National Christmas Tree, a thirty-four-foot Colorado blue spruce from Maryland, and his wife oversaw the decorating of the mansion. Her Blue Room tree featured painted milkweed pods, nut pods, foil and eggshell ornaments made by disabled members of the National Association for Retarded Citizens.

A few days later, on December 22, the Carters went home for the holidays. For the first time ever, he would spend Christmas in his hometown of Plains, Georgia, as the president of the United States. It was a place that brought back many memories because he had grown up there during the Great Depression.

President Carter recalled that period, "The Great Depression was a time of almost incredible poverty, not only in Southwest Georgia but all over the country. Although my father was a landowner, money was scarce for us and everybody else."

He grew up on his parent's peanut farm and earned money by picking the crop and selling bags to the townspeople. As a youngster, the family would celebrate Christmas but without expensive gifts and huge trees. Jimmy and his father Earl would search their land for a sturdy wild red cedar tree which they would remove from the forest and bring back to the house.

Once they brought the tree home, it was time to decorate it but that didn't mean they used fancy store bought ornaments. The family made their own decorations using things like tin foil and strings of popcorn and berries. There were no Christmas lights because, like most of the houses in the area, the Carters had no electricity. They also had no indoor plumbing.

Because they lived on a farm, chores needed to be done even if it was Christmas Day. So, the family went about caring for their animals, toting buckets of water to the house, and collecting firewood for heating and cooking. To celebrate the holiday in the evening, many of those living in the area would light fireworks. There were four stands in Plains where local citizens could buy them at cheap prices.

There weren't many gifts but Jimmy always asked for books. He loved to read and was quite good at it. Additionally, even though he grew up in a house without electricity, he was an outstanding student in school.

When the president, his wife, and ten-year-old daughter Amy returned to Plains for the holidays in 1977, things were quite different from when he lived there. First of all, he had owned the family peanut business for several years and made it very successful. The president no longer lived on the farm but in a nice home, with electricity and plumbing, in the downtown area. Also, when he returned to his hometown, he was tracked by a large group of Secret Service agents who followed him everywhere.

That year, the Carters set a record by ordering and sending out 60,000 Christmas cards. That was more than any previous administration. That number continued to increase over the next three years.

At the end of his term in 1981, the Carters returned to Plains where they still live today. Every Christmas they gather with their four adult children and their many grandchildren and great-grandchildren but, unlike when the former president was a boy, no one has to go collect water or firewood for the holiday.

Today's Questions

1. President Carter grew up in the town of Plains. In what state is Plains located?
   (A) Texas   (B) Oklahoma   (C) Georgia
2. What was the main crop that was raised on the Carter's family farm?
3. What did the people of Plains use to celebrate Christmas in the evening?

It's a Fact . . .

In 1977, there was a news story where one of Amy Carter's friends said that she wanted a chainsaw for Christmas because, "she likes the way they work."

A few days later, a package arrived at the White House from the Greenwood Saw Company in South Carolina that contained a brand-new chainsaw. Being that she was the daughter of the American president, it was colored red, white, and blue. Although thoughtful, the Carters felt that Amy was too young to handle such a machine and she was not allowed to keep it.

Yes, it's true!

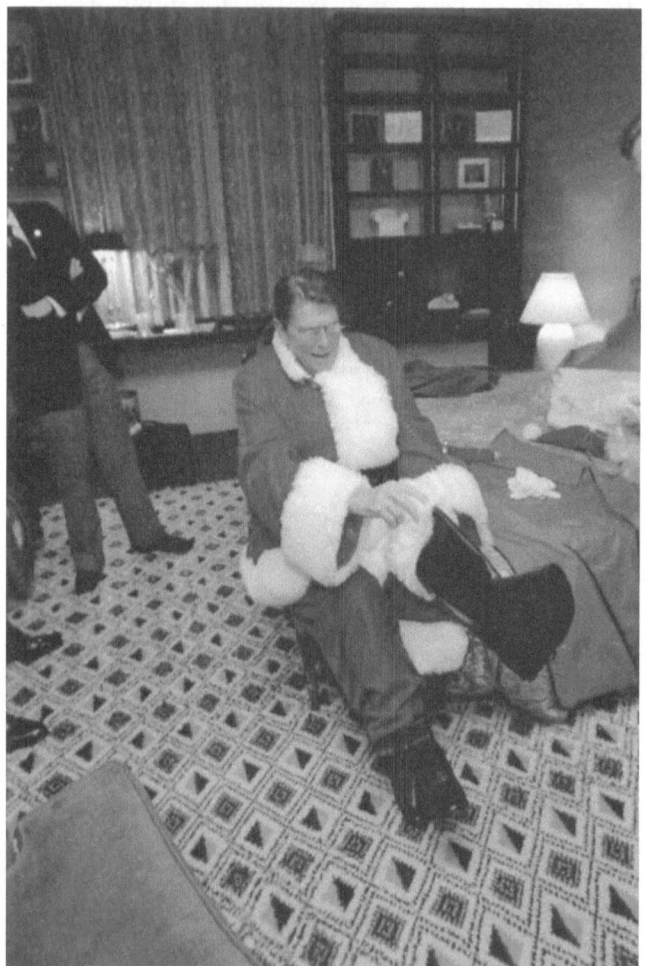

Here comes Santa Claus! Not really, it's President Ronald Reagan putting on the famous suit for a friend's party (Ronald Reagan Presidential Library and Museum photo).

Chapter 37

Ronald Reagan
The 40th President
The Meaning of Christmas

In 1980, President Jimmy Carter was running for reelection. His opponent was the former governor of California Ronald Reagan. Each of the men had a very different idea about how the business of running the United States should be conducted. In the end, the voters chose Mr. Reagan.

Although they didn't agree about politics, there was one area where the two men were very much alike. Like former President Carter, Ronald Reagan had gone through some difficult times growing up during the Great Depression. His boyhood years were spent in Dixon, Illinois, where, like many of their friends, the Reagans had very little money. There were times when young Ron and his older brother Neil had to depend on the goodness of their neighbors in order to get a meal because their parents couldn't afford to buy food.

The Reagans were so poor that they never had a true Christmas celebration like other families.

"There were very few decorated trees in the years of my growing up," President Reagan recalled. "But never defeated, my mother would, with ribbon and crepe paper, decorate a table or create a cardboard fireplace out of a packing box. And she always remembered whose birthday it was and made sure we knew the meaning of Christmas."

However, the family's most difficult time came in 1931 on Christmas Eve.

President Reagan would tell the story to crowds during his campaign for president, "Back in those dark depression days, I saw my father on a Christmas Eve open what he thought was a Christmas greeting from his boss. Instead, it was the blue slip telling him he no longer had a job. The memory of him sitting there holding that slip of paper and then saying in a half whisper, 'That's quite a Christmas present,' will stay with me as long as I live."

But the hard times didn't stop Ronald Reagan; in fact, they made him more determined to be successful. He graduated from college and then became a radio sportscaster. From there, he traveled to Hollywood becoming a well-known movie and television actor. During his years in acting, Mr. Reagan made a lot of money so his children never faced the hardships that he had during the Depression and they always had gifts for Christmas.

In 1981, President Reagan started a new tradition approving the creation of the first official White House Christmas ornament. Since then, a new decoration design is offered each year that can be bought by the public. The money raised from the sale of the ornaments is used to preserve the historic rooms of the White House.

That same year, First Lady Nancy Reagan threw a special Christmas party for 178 hearing-impaired children. They enjoyed the acts of entertainers who were also unable to hear.

Mr. Reagan was president for eight years and each was celebrated with a grand celebration. Because he had been an actor, it wasn't unusual for celebrities to drop by the White House for a holiday party. In 1983, action television star Mr. T dressed as Santa Claus for one of those gatherings. A few days later, the president decided to join the fun and put on the Santa suit for a friend's Christmas Eve party.

Away from the White House, President Reagan owned a large horse ranch in the Santa Barbara Mountains of California. He and Mrs. Reagan enjoyed spending as much time there as possible. But not at Christmas.

Rather than travel during the holidays, the Reagans chose to stay in Washington, D.C., to allow the Secret Service agents and other aides the chance to spend Christmas at home with their families. That was their special gift to those who had done so much for them.

TODAY'S QUESTIONS

1. President Reagan grew up in this state.
   (A) New York   (B) Indiana   (C) Illinois
2. What happened to President Reagan's father on Christmas Eve in 1931?
3. Why did the Reagans stay in Washington, D.C., during the Christmas holidays?

It's a Fact

Have you ever received or has your family ever bought a computer for Christmas? The electronic gadget became popular in the 1980s when Ronald Reagan was president and since then, millions have been given as holiday gifts.

Also, the most wanted computer game of the 1980s was Pac-Man. Just how popular was it? By 1990, it had earned an amazing $2.5 billion!

Yes, it's true!

First Lady Barbara Bush and her granddaughter top the National Tree. November 27, 1989 (whitehouse.gov photo).

CHAPTER 38

George H.W. Bush
The 41st President
A Cherry Picker for Christmas

Christmas is a special time of the year for most people but it has extra meaning for former president George H.W. Bush and his wife Barbara. That's because, many decades ago, they met during the holiday season for the first time.

In December 1941, seventeen-year-old George and sixteen-year-old Barbara were attending a dance in his hometown of Greenwich, Connecticut, during the Christmas break from school. She was from the town of Rye in nearby New York and they've both described that meeting as love at first sight.

The teenagers began dating but there was a problem. The United States entered World War II during the same month that George and Barbara had met. The following June, after his high school graduation, he joined the U.S. Navy and trained to be a pilot. George flew fifty-eight combat missions in the Pacific and, in 1944, became the youngest pilot to be shot down by the enemy.

During his time in the military, Barbara wrote to the naval lieutenant almost every day. They were engaged while he was still in the service and were married in 1945, a short time after he returned home.

During more than seventy years of marriage, they raised five children. George became a successful businessman in Texas and started getting into politics in 1964. He held several different jobs in government service, in fact, he had so many positions that he and his family moved an amazing twenty-nine times!

But his biggest move came in January 1989 when he was sworn in as the forty-first president of the United States and began living in the White

House. Like most of the nation's leaders, Mr. Bush stayed busy tending to the problems of the country and the world. Meanwhile, Mrs. Bush took over the duties of preparing the mansion for the holidays.

However, the First Lady had established a new tradition eight years earlier while her husband was the vice president. As the National Community Christmas Tree was nearly finished being decorated, Mrs. Bush would climb into a cherry picker to be taken to the top of the tall timber. A cherry picker is a crane with a metal bucket on the end to raise and lower people, usually those who are working in high places such as overhead signs or street lights. The machine would take her to the top of the tree which was thirty feet above the ground where she would place a large star on its top branch.

Mrs. Bush was very active in programs to help children learning to read. In 1989, she worked that program into the White House Christmas theme as she presented a "Storybook Christmas" featuring figures of famous children's book characters such as Aladdin and Babar. That year, the presents under the trees were books tied up with red bows.

The First Lady also hosted a special party for homeless children from the Central Union Mission in Washington, D.C. She spent time presenting gift bags filled with presents and then read Christmas stories to the youngsters. Mrs. Bush followed a history of other First Ladies who helped homeless children in the nation's capital at Christmas.

Like the Reagans, the Bushes chose to remain near the White House over the holidays. During the four-year term, they spent Christmas at Camp David in Maryland. It is the official getaway place for the First Family and is only about sixty-five miles from Washington, D.C. Joining them for Christmas were their adult children with their families which included several grandchildren.

In 1990, while members of the Bush family enjoyed the holiday season at Camp David, the president was busy with other matters. Months earlier, on the other side of the world, the country of Iraq invaded its neighbor Kuwait. Kuwait is a very small country without much of a military to defend itself. They are also a friend of the United States.

President Bush spent much of his Christmas vacation trying to decide whether or not to send American troops to the area to rescue Kuwait. It was an important decision. Three weeks later, U.S. forces arrived in the Middle East to remove Iraq's army from the tiny nation. It took six weeks, but the Americans drove the enemy out of Kuwait and allowed them to, once again, enjoy their freedom.

To this day, President George H.W. Bush is celebrated as a national hero in the nation of Kuwait.

In 1992, for their final White House holiday, the Bushes ordered 185,000 Christmas cards. That was the most greeting cards ever ordered by a First Family to that point in history.

TODAY'S QUESTIONS

1. George Bush was a pilot during World War II. In what branch of the military did he serve?
   (A) Army   (B) Navy   (C) Marines
2. What type of machine took Barbara Bush to the top of the National Community Christmas Tree where she placed a star?
3. Which nation did President Bush help after they were invaded by Iraq?
   (A) Kuwait   (B) Canada   (C) Spain

IT'S A FACT . . .

Most people know that Barbara Bush is married to a president (George H.W. Bush), that's no surprise. They are also aware that her son, George W. Bush, also became president.

What a number of citizens are not aware of is that the former First Lady is related to another president.

Before marrying Mr. Bush, her maiden name was Barbara Pierce and she is the fourth cousin four times removed to President Franklin Perce, who you read about in chapter 13. He was the first president to decorate a Christmas tree on the White House grounds.

That means that Barbara Bush is the only person in U.S. history to be a wife, a mother, and a cousin to three former presidents.

Yes, it's true!

President Bill Clinton greets U.S. troops at Sarajevo in Bosnia and Herzegovina on December 22, 1995 (United States Department of Defense photo).

CHAPTER 39

Bill Clinton
The 42nd President
Peace on Earth

One of the most famous Christmas phrases is, "Peace on earth, good will to men." Unfortunately, during every holiday season, there are places throughout the world where there is more fighting than friendship.

This was on Bill Clinton's mind when he became president in January 1993. Many times, the leader of the United States is looked upon as the person to help bring peace to other parts of the world. In early December 1995, while many Americans were doing their Christmas shopping, President Clinton and his wife, First Lady Hillary, arrived in the country of Northern Ireland. It was the first time that the leader of the U.S. had visited that European nation.

However, it wasn't a vacation trip as this was a dangerous situation for the Clintons because the country had been dealing with their own version of a civil war for almost thirty years. That night, in a historic moment of peace in the capital city of Belfast, the president lit the city's Christmas tree. The huge crowd cheered loudly as many waved American flags. His visit to the country was a small step but it gave many Irish citizens hope for a lasting peace.

Two years later, in 1997, President Clinton continued the annual tradition of lighting Washington, D.C.'s National Christmas Tree. He also started a new custom by being the first U.S. president to perform a candle lighting of a menorah in the White House. This is done to mark the start of Hanukkah, the eight-day Jewish Festival of Lights. Every president since then has also lit a menorah inside the mansion.

President Clinton was busy following the celebrations in the nation's capital; he was off again to another part of the world.

On December 22, 1997, just three days before Christmas, the president was joined by Mrs. Clinton and their seventeen-year-old daughter Chelsea on a journey to the city of Sarajevo (pronounced Sara-ya-vo) in the country of Bosnia-Herzegovina. Earlier that year, he had made the decision to send U.S. troops to help the nation which was at war. The holiday visit gave President Clinton a chance to meet with his generals as to the progress of their mission.

During a speech to the citizens in Sarajevo, the president told them, "In the end, the future is up to you, not to the Americans, not to the Europeans, not to anyone else. What I want all of you to believe today is that you can do it."

When the Clintons returned to the mansion for Christmas, there was a new family member who was there to greet them. The president's new dog, three-month-old Buddy, was enjoying his first holiday. The family had bought the puppy shortly before their trip to Sarajevo but he did not travel with them.

In December 1998, the Clintons hosted a concert at the White House called *A Very Special Christmas Live*. It included many of the top recording artists of that time. The event was recorded and the money that was raised from the sales of the CD was donated to the Special Olympics.

Shortly before Christmas during Bill Clinton's final year as president in 2000, he returned to Northern Ireland and found it to be a much different than the place he had visited five years earlier. The main reason was that the country was at peace and the United States had helped create the end of the years of violence by helping work out the terms of the treaty. One of the reasons that peace in the region was so important to the Clintons was that his great-great grandparents had been born in Ireland.

While they were well known, the truth was that during their eight Christmas seasons at the White House, the First Family weren't the stars of the show. That honor went to their pet cat Socks. The popular feline could often be seen running through the mansion and was a favorite with visiting children. In 1993, the White House chef made a gingerbread house called the "House of Socks," showing America's most famous cat playing twenty-one different characters. It took the chef 150 hours to create the elaborate dessert!

TODAY'S QUESTIONS

1. What did President Clinton do in Northern Ireland that made the people cheer in the city of Belfast?
2. What group received the money from the sale of the C.D., "A Very Special Christmas Live?"

3. What did the White House chef create to honor the Clinton's cat, Socks?

It's a Fact . . .

There are many people who wait until the last minute to do their Christmas shopping and President Clinton was one of them. It was not unusual to see him, joined by his Secret Service agents, making his way through stores in Washington, D.C., on Christmas Eve.

But that changed in 1999 as the nation's leader joined millions of other Americans and, for the first time, did his holiday shopping over the Internet.

Yes, it's true!

The 2001 National Christmas Tree with its patriotic theme (White House photo by Susan Sterner).

Chapter 40

George W. Bush
The 43rd President
Remembrance and Goodwill

George W. Bush understood how tough the job would be when he was elected president of the United States in 2000. That's because he had worked closely with his father who had held the same position eight years earlier. They were the second father and son to be elected to the nation's highest office. John Adams and his son John Quincy had been the first.

But perhaps no president in history had a more difficult first year in office than George W. Bush. That's because on September 11, 2001, New York City and Washington, D.C., were attacked by terrorists. Almost 3,000 people died on that day and another 6,000 were injured. For the leader of the country, his worst nightmare had come true.

The invasion changed the way that Christmas would be celebrated that year. Normally, large crowds toured the White House to view the holiday displays and decorations. But because of the fear of another attack, all visits by the public were canceled. Also, Pennsylvania Avenue, the large street that runs directly in front of the mansion, was closed to cars and other vehicles.

But First Lady Laura Bush was determined not to let the terrorists ruin Christmas for the citizens. For that year's theme, she chose Home for the Holidays and said, "Because this year's holiday season follows a national tragedy, both home and family have special meaning to all Americans. Gatherings of loved ones—familiar faces in familiar places—can be a tremendous source of strength and reassurance during this season of remembrance and goodwill."

Artists from all fifty states and the District of Columbia designed model replicas of historic homes and houses of worship to hang as ornaments.

On December 6, President Bush lit the National Christmas Tree which, as usual, was broadcast on television. There were some on his security team who believed that holding the annual ceremony would be too dangerous but the president stood firm. He even had the tree's traditional seasonal color scheme of red, green, and gold changed to the country's national colors that included red garland; 100,000 white and blue lights; and 100 white star ornaments. The tree topper was a huge patriotic star.

The president and First Lady were joined at the lighting honors by five-year-old Leon Patterson and six-year-old Faith Elseth whose fathers had been victims of the September 11 attack in Washington, D.C. The evening concluded with entertainment by a number of celebrities and a guest appearance by Santa Claus.

A few days later, the Bushes left the White House to join their family for the holidays. Like his parents, the president chose to spend Christmas at nearby Camp David so that his staff and Secret Service agents could be with their families who lived in the area. It had been a very busy year for the protective team of the First Family.

With all of the activity of 9/11, extra security was assigned to President and Mrs. Bush. The agents were also responsible for the safety of the couple's twin daughters, Barbara and Jenna, who were away at college. It is true that the children of the president also receive protection from the Secret Service.

Do you believe that the children of the president need to be protected?

As time passed, life across the United States began to return to almost normal as in 2003, the popular tours of the White House resumed including those during the holiday season. There was also another tradition that continued and became bigger.

You might remember that in 1953, President Eisenhower sent out 1,000 White House Christmas cards. By the time that the Bushes celebrated their final holiday at the mansion in 2008, they sent a record 2.25 million cards to friends and associates. That's a lot of friends!

Today's Questions

1. Who was the first father and son to both be elected president of the United States?
2. President Bush changed the colors of the National Christmas Tree for 2001. What were the three new colors?
3. True or False—The children of the president of United States also receive Secret Service protection?

It's a Fact . . .

In 2002, due to the added security precautions from the 9/11 attacks, many members of the public were unable to visit the White House to view its holiday decorations. Because of that, Mrs. Bush came up with an idea.

She placed a small camera on the collar of the family's Scottish Terrier Barney and then allowed him to roam through the White House as it was recording. Barney's film was turned into a four and a half minute video tour of the decorated mansion. It was broadcast on the White House website and received 24 million views on its first day. The feature became so popular that Mrs. Bush repeated the process with a new Barney Cam Christmas tour for each of the next six years.

Yes, it's true!

President Obama takes care of some business in the Oval Office during the 2010 Christmas season (whitehouse.gov photo, Pete Souza).

Chapter 41

Barack Obama
The 44th President
The Christmas Letter

In 2014, thirteen-year-old Malik Bryant was a seventh grader who lived on the south side of Chicago. Unfortunately, he and his mother resided in one of the city's roughest neighborhoods known as Englewood. It is a place with a great deal of crime and gang activity. Most of the area is too dangerous for kids to play outside.

That year, Malik wrote a letter to Santa through a local charity to tell him what he wanted for Christmas. This was not a request for toys, games, a computer, or any of the things that one might expect. Instead he wrote, "All I ask for is for safety. I just want to be safe."

It was just one of more than 8,000 letters received at the charity's headquarters. The head of the organization was a woman named Michelle who was impressed with Malik's request but didn't actually know what to do next. She made some phone calls and a few days later, Malik received a reply to his letter but it wasn't from Santa. It was from a man who had lived in Chicago for seventeen years. The letter read as follows:

"I want to offer you a few words of encouragement. Each day, I strive to ensure communities like yours are safe places to dream, discover, and grow. Please know your security is a priority for me in everything I do as President. If you dare to be bold and creative, work hard every day, and care for others, I'm confident you can achieve anything you imagine. I wish you and your family the very best for the coming year, and I will be rooting for you."

It was signed, President Barack Obama.

Malik wasn't the only one who hoped for the violence to end in Chicago; millions of Americans throughout the nation also shared his dream.

One month later, he flew to Washington, D.C., as the guest of the First Lady to attend the president's annual State of the Union speech. The young man has said that he hopes to someday attend college and perhaps play basketball.

TODAY'S QUESTIONS

1. What is the name of the city where Malik lives?
2. What did Malik tell Santa in his letter that he wanted for Christmas?
3. Who sent Malik a reply to his letter?

IT'S A FACT . . .

Atlanta is the capital city of the state of Georgia. The average temperature there on December 25 is a pleasant fifty-two degrees. But something strange took place on Christmas Day in 2010 while Barack Obama was president.

For the first time since 1882, it snowed in Atlanta. It wasn't a large amount, just one to three inches, but combined with the ice on the ground, it made driving conditions dangerous on the city's streets.

Also, hundreds of airline flights were canceled due to the weather which forced many travelers to spend Christmas Day at Atlanta's airport.

Yes, it's true!

Chapter 42

Donald Trump
The 45th President
The Gift of Giving

In November 2016, the voters across America gave Donald Trump a gift. They made him the forty-fifth president of the United States. But long before he moved into the White House, he realized that it is better to give than to receive.

Perhaps that's because Mr. Trump is different from any of our nation's leaders from the past. Before he became a politician, he was known as one of the top builders of expensive hotels and golf courses throughout the world and, by doing that, he became rich. When he won the election in 2016, he was worth around $4 billion making him the wealthiest president in the history of the country!

While he sometimes comes across as a tough guy when he appears on television, there is another side to the billionaire that many people don't usually get to see

In 1986, a sixty-six-year-old woman named Annabel, who lived in Georgia, was about to lose her family's farm because her husband had died and she hadn't been able to keep up with the payments. She owed more than $100,000 to the bank that was about to take over her home and land.

"I saw a story on the news about Annabel Hill, who'd hit bottom," said the president. "It was a very sad situation, and I was moved. Here were people who'd worked very hard and honestly all their lives, only to see it all crumble before them. To me, it just seemed wrong."

Mr. Trump teamed up with another businessman to stop the takeover. They paid off the bank and got Annabel's farm back for her. She said about the act of kindness shown by the businessman, "the only way I can explain it was God touched his heart."

There was another situation in 1986 that needed Mr. Trump's attention. One of the most famous places in his hometown of New York City is Central Park, a spot where in the winter, many residents and visitors enjoy ice skating. But the old rink was in need of repairs and the project was going nowhere.

The city had been trying to fix the skating location for six years and had spent more than $12 million but still wasn't finished. At that point, Mr. Trump told the city's officials that he could have the job done by Christmas for a lot less money. They gave him the go ahead to take over the project.

His crew went to work and completed the work by early November and had saved the city thousands of dollars. When it was done, Trump's workers had built the largest man-made skating rink in the world. People flocked to the area to enjoy holiday ice skating in Central Park and continue to do so today.

But perhaps the greatest gift that the former businessman gave was in 1988 when he helped save the life of a three-year-old boy. The youngster was named Andrew and he lived in Los Angeles with his parents. He suffered from a rare illness and needed to travel to New York City for special treatment.

Unfortunately, none of the airlines could have him as a passenger because of all of the equipment and machines that were being used to help keep him alive. When Donald Trump was contacted and told about Andrew, he volunteered to send his private plane to pick up the boy, his family, along with all of the equipment and bring them 3,000 miles to New York.

When the plane arrived with Andrew, he was quickly taken to the hospital where he received special care from the doctors and nurses. He lived another ten years and his family has always been grateful to President Trump for coming to their son's rescue.

Christmas truly is the season of giving.

Today's Questions

1. How did President Trump make so much money?
2. Where was the ice skating rink that President Trump had repaired?
3. What did President Trump do to help Andrew?

President Donald J. Trump (photo by Gage Skidmore).

IT'S A FACT . . .

In 1992, before he was president, Mr. Trump made a guest appearance in the hit holiday movie, *Home Alone* 2. The scene was filmed in the lobby of the Plaza Hotel in New York City which he owned at the time.

Yes, it's true!

A team of volunteers decorates the official White House Christmas Tree in the Blue Room of the White House in 2009 (official White House photo).

Chapter 43

That Special Time of the Year
White House Christmas Themes

In 1961, Jacqueline Kennedy started the tradition of First Ladies selecting the official theme for the White House Christmas. She began the custom with decorations modeled after Pyotr Ilyich Tchaikovsky's ballet, *The Nutcracker Suite*. This annual celebration of the holidays continues to this day.

YEAR	THEME	FIRST LADY
1961	"The Nutcracker Suite"	Jacqueline Kennedy
The first of what became the annual theme selected by the First Lady.		
1962	"The Christmas Tree"	Jacqueline Kennedy
The wonder of Christmas as seen through the eyes of children.		
1963	"Journey of the Magi and an Angel"	Jacqueline Kennedy
Although by Christmas she was no longer the First Lady, Mrs. Kennedy had already selected the Christmas theme for 1963 prior to President Kennedy's death.		
1964–1968	"Early America"	Claudia "Lady Bird" Johnson
The Johnson theme was based on an early American theme featuring nuts, popcorn, fruit, wood roses from Hawaii, a paper mâché angel, and gingerbread cookies. In 1967 and 1968, Mrs. Johnson expanded the theme by adding felt flowers remaining from her daughter's wedding.		

YEAR	THEME	FIRST LADY
1969–1970	"State Flower Balls"	Patricia Nixon

For the decorations of the White House tree, First Lady Patricia Nixon arranged for disabled workers in Florida to make velvet and satin balls featuring each state's flower. The following year, she added fifty-three "Monroe" gold foil fans.

1971	"Gold Foil Angels"	Patricia Nixon

Mrs. Nixon added gold-foiled angels to the previous year's decorations.

1972	"Nature's Bounty"	Patricia Nixon

The chosen theme was inspired by German American artist, Severin Roesen and his works, *Still Life with Fruit and Nature's Bounty*. The tree featured 3,000 pastel satin-finish balls, the state flower balls, and 150 gold Federal stars.

1973	"James Monroe"	Patricia Nixon

Lots of gold ornaments and decorations were used to honor the nation's fifth president.

1974	"Patchwork Christmas"	Betty Ford

Mrs. Ford's theme was highlighted by thrift and recycling using ornaments made by Appalachian women and senior citizens groups.

1975	"Children's Christmas"	Betty Ford

The theme was sponsored by the Colonial Williamsburg Foundation and the Abby Aldrich Folk Art Museum.

1976	"America Is Love"	Betty Ford

This was also the year of the nation's Bicentennial.

1977	"Classic American Christmas"	Rosalynn Carter

Mrs. Carter used natural elements such as wood, pine cones, peanuts, and eggshells in many of the decorations. She also had some of the ornaments crafted by members of the National Association for Retarded Citizens.

1978	"Antique Toys"	Rosalynn Carter

The Margaret Woodbury Strong Museum loaned the White House over 2,500 antique toys for their display.

1979	"American Folk Art of the Colonial Period"	Rosalynn Carter

The theme featured ornaments created by students of the Corcoran School of Art in Washington, D.C.

1980	"Old Fashion Victorian Christmas"	Rosalynn Carter

The theme's designer, Master Craftsman Louis Nichole, used dolls, dollhouses, and children's toys for the display.

YEAR	THEME	FIRST LADY
1981	"Old Fashion Christmas with the Museum of Folk Art"	Nancy Reagan
That year's theme featured treasures, many in wood, from the Museum of American Folk Art in New York.		
1982	"Old Fashion Christmas with Foil Paper Cones and Snowflakes"	Nancy Reagan
The featured items were cones made from foil paper and metallic snowflakes.		
1983	"Old Fashion Christmas with Antique Toys"	Nancy Reagan
An antique toy circus beneath the tree was the main attraction. Once again, old-fashioned toys were lent by the Margaret Woodbury Strong Museum.		
1984	"Enchanting Creatures"	Nancy Reagan
That year included offerings from the Brandywine River Museum in Pennsylvania which displayed hand-crafted Christmas animals made from natural materials.		
1985	"Old Fashion Christmas with Teddy Bears"	Nancy Reagan
The famous toy named after President Theodore Roosevelt was the star of the show.		
1986	"Mother Goose"	Nancy Reagan
The display included fifteen soft-sculpture nursery rhyme scenes and 100 geese for a "Mother Goose" tree.		
1987	"Toyland Musical Tree"	Nancy Reagan
Miniature instruments could be seen by visitors who toured the mansion that year.		
1988	"Old Fashion Christmas"	Nancy Reagan
White House carpenters made 300 wood candles for the 1988 Blue Room tree.		
1989	"Storybook Christmas"	Barbara Bush
Mrs. Bush's first White House Christmas during her husband's presidency featured characters from children's books and accented them with gold and red ribbon.		
1990	"The Nutcracker Suite"	Barbara Bush
Mrs. Bush revisited the characters used by Jacqueline Kennedy for the first White House–themed Christmas in 1961.		
1991	"Needlepoint Christmas"	Barbara Bush
Many of the needlepoint decorations were done by Mrs. Bush's friends back in Houston. To give it a Texas twist, they included armadillos to the Nativity scene.		
1992	"Gift Givers"	Barbara Bush
There was no shortage of Santa Claus, Kris Kringle, and the Snow Maid at the 1992 display.		

YEAR	THEME	FIRST LADY
1993	"Angels and the Year of the American Craft"	Hillary Rodham Clinton
Angels were made by various artists using different mediums such as wood, metal, fiberglass, clay, and needlepoint.		
1994	"Twelve Days of Christmas"	Hillary Rodham Clinton
Decoration duties were handled by the legendary designer Ralph Lauren using red and green tartan ribbon trimmings.		
1995	"A Visit from Saint Nicholas"	Hillary Rodham Clinton
This theme was inspired by the poem, "The Night before Christmas"		
1996	"The Nutcracker Suite"	Hillary Rodham Clinton
Mrs. Clinton became the third First Lady to use the popular Nutcracker theme.		
1997	"Santa's Workshop"	Hillary Rodham Clinton
Glass artists, needlepointers, and fashion designers along with members of the Council of Fashion Designers of America put together a replica of the most famous workshop for all to see.		
1998	"Winter Wonderland"	Hillary Rodham Clinton
One group of ornaments was designed by artists based on the recommendations of the governors' spouses in each of the fifty states.		
1999	"Holiday Treasures at the White House"	Hillary Rodham Clinton
The theme featured decorations that highlighted famous landmarks, people, and historical events. Included were eighty handmade dolls of well-known Americans such as Sacajawea, Benjamin Franklin, Rosa Parks, and Amelia Earhart.		
2000	"Holiday Reflections"	Hillary Rodham Clinton
A combination of items that featured all of the past White House Christmases of the Clinton's.		
2001	"Home for the Holidays"	Laura Bush
For the ornaments, artists from all fifty states and the District of Columbia designed miniature replicas of historic houses from their regions.		
2002	"All Creatures Great and Small"	Laura Bush
The exhibit featured twenty-five paper-mâché sculptures of America's presidential pets crafted by White House staffers. The animals included raccoons and sheep, as well as the famous alligator that belonged to John Quincy Adams, which decorated mantles and tables throughout the mansion. Red and gold was the primary color scheme.		

YEAR	THEME	FIRST LADY
2003	"Season of Stories"	Laura Bush
The First Lady was a former librarian, so that year's theme centered on classic children's stories and characters, including Clifford the Big Red Dog, The Cat in the Hat, The Polar Express, and Harry Potter.		
2004	"Season of Merriment and Melody"	Laura Bush
The theme featured icicle trees and holiday musical favorites.		
2005	"All Things Bright and Beautiful"	Laura Bush
Mrs. Bush chose to highlight the beauty to be found in nature with the focus on the many ways the plants, trees, fruit, and flowers can play a major role in holiday decorating.		
2006	"Deck the Halls and Welcome All"	Laura Bush
The theme featured elegant beads and glass ornaments recalling historic holiday memories at the White House.		
2007	"Holiday in the National Parks"	Laura Bush
The country's national parks and monuments took center stage at the White House.		
2008	"Red, White, and Blue Christmas"	Laura Bush
For the Bush's final White House Christmas, a theme with flags and oversized nutcrackers was chosen.		
2009	"Reflect, Rejoice, and Renew"	Michelle Obama
The Obama's first Christmas at the mansion was set up with the help of members of the White House staff along with ninety-two volunteers from twenty-four states who spent more than 3,400 hours getting the White House ready for the holidays.		
2010	"Simple Gifts"	Michelle Obama
The theme included a tribute to the five branches of the United States military.		
2011	"Shine, Share, Give"	Michelle Obama
The theme's message was spending time with friends and family, celebrating the joy of giving to others, and sharing one's blessings with all.		
2012	"Joy to All"	Michelle Obama
The joy of giving and service to others served as that year's theme.		
2013	"Gather Around: Stories of the Season"	Michelle Obama
A celebration of the stories and traditions of the holiday season. Twenty-four trees throughout the White House were used to tell a story.		

YEAR	THEME	FIRST LADY
2014	"A Children's Wonderland"	Michelle Obama
Creative visuals, custom ornaments, and graphic expressions turned the White House into a magical place.		
2015	"A Timeless Tradition"	Michelle Obama
That year's White House decorations paid tribute to the Armed Forces and their families. They included a handcrafted 500-pound gingerbread house, sixty-two fir trees, and 70,000 ornaments.		
2016	"The Gift of the Holidays"	Michelle Obama
The theme of the Obama's final White House Christmas celebrated family and friends, reflection and remembrance, along with excitement and cheer.		

The History of the National Christmas Tree

Each year, a tree is chosen for the honor of serving as the National Tree. Part of the display of decorations are the fifty special ornaments that represent each state. When the president turns on the lights, it signals to everyone that the Christmas season has officially begun.

Inside the White House, the traditional tree is erected in the Blue Room while another is placed upstairs in the First Family's living quarters. Since 1966, members of the National Christmas Tree Association have presented a fresh Christmas tree that is displayed in the Blue Room.

In 1923, the first National Christmas Tree Lighting Ceremony was held.

YEAR	TYPE OF TREE	HOME STATE	HEIGHT	PRESIDENT
1923	Balsam Fir	Vermont	48'	Calvin Coolidge
This tree was donated by Paul D. Moody, president of Middlebury College in President Coolidge's home state of Vermont.				
1924–1927	Norway Spruce	New York	35'	Calvin Coolidge
This was the first living timber used as the National Christmas Tree.				
1928–1930	Norway Spruce	New York	35'	Herbert Hoover
The first living tree, planted in 1924, was found to be damaged due to the process of trimming and the repeated stress caused by the heat and weight of the lights. Both the 1924 and 1928 trees were donated by the American Forestry Association and the Amawalk Tree Farm in Yorktown, New York.				

That Special Time of the Year

YEAR	TYPE OF TREE	HOME STATE	HEIGHT	PRESIDENT
1931–1933	Blue Spruce	Washington, D.C.	25'	Herbert Hoover (1931–1932) Franklin D. Roosevelt (1933)
This was another replacement tree as the previous one was discovered to have been damaged.				
1934–1938	Fraser Fir*	North Carolina	23'	Franklin D. Roosevelt
There were technical difficulties during the 1934 ceremony. When the magic moment arrived, President Roosevelt pressed the button but the lights didn't turn on. He looked around for help for several seconds and then the colorful bulbs flashed on throughout the tree.				
1939	Red Cedar	Virginia	36'	Franklin D. Roosevelt
1940	Red Cedar	Virginia	34'	Franklin D. Roosevelt
The 1939 and 1940 trees were retrieved from Virginia's Mount Vernon Memorial Highway, just a short distance from George Washington's home.				
1941–1953	Oriental Spruce*	Washington, D.C.	35'	Franklin D. Roosevelt (1941–1944); Harry Truman (1945–1952); Dwight D. Eisenhower (1953)
In honor of those serving in the military during World War II, the National Tree was not lit in 1942, 1943, and 1944.				
1954	Balsam Fir	Michigan	67'	Dwight D. Eisenhower
For the first time, the lighting of the National Christmas Tree did not occur on Christmas Eve. It took place on December 17 because the organizers wanted more time to celebrate the holidays. The idea became so popular that it continues that way today.				
1955	White Spruce	South Dakota	67'	Dwight D. Eisenhower
This was the first tree to be used that was grown west of the Mississippi River.				
1956	Engelmann Spruce	New Mexico	67'3"	Dwight D. Eisenhower
This big tree was decorated with 5,000 lights, 4,000 decorations, and 1,000 ornaments.				

YEAR	TYPE OF TREE	HOME STATE	HEIGHT	PRESIDENT
1957	White Spruce	Minnesota	60'	Dwight D. Eisenhower
In a number of the nation's larger cities, the mayors timed their tree lightings to correspond with the national tree in Washington, D.C.				
1958	Engelmann Spruce	Montana	75'	Dwight D. Eisenhower
Ten live reindeer took part in the ceremony. They were a gift to President Eisenhower and the nation from the governor and citizens of Alaska, which became America's forty-ninth state just three weeks later.				
1959	White Spruce	Maine	72'	Dwight D. Eisenhower
The tree was from the Elmbrook farm of Miss Alice Kimball in Presque Isle, Maine. It was the first National Christmas Tree that came from a private citizen. It was estimated to be over 100 years old, had a diameter at the base of twenty-two inches with a branch spread of approximately twenty-eight feet. The weight of the tree was estimated to exceed three tons.				
1960	Douglas Fir	Oregon	75'	Dwight D. Eisenhower
This was the first National Christmas Tree from the Pacific Coast.				
1961	Douglas Fir	Washington	75'	John F. Kennedy
The tree was lit with 3,000 lights that were synchronized to music which meant that when the songs began to play, the lights would flicker.				
1962	Blue Spruce	Colorado	72'	John F. Kennedy
This was the only year that President Kennedy lit the National Christmas tree at the Pageant of Peace. He had missed the 1961 ceremony to be with his father who was ill.				
1963	Red Spruce	West Virginia	71'	Lyndon B. Johnson
The lighting of the tree was delayed an additional four days to December 22 to mark the end of the thirty-day mourning period following the death of President Kennedy.				
1964	White Spruce	New York	72'	Lyndon B. Johnson
Following the lighting of the tree there was a lunar eclipse.				
1965	Blue Spruce	Arizona	85'	Lyndon B. Johnson
The tree came from Arizona's White Mountain Apache Indian Reservation. It was the first tree from a Native American tribe for use as the National Christmas Tree.				
1966	Red Fir	California	65'	Lyndon B. Johnson

That Special Time of the Year

YEAR	TYPE OF TREE	HOME STATE	HEIGHT	PRESIDENT
Seated near President Johnson at the ceremony were four U.S. astronauts. He was a big supporter of the space program.				
1967	Balsam Fir	Vermont	70'	Lyndon B. Johnson
President Johnson brought his mixed-breed dog Yuki to the ceremony. The little pet wore a red cap and a white beard.				
1968	Engelmann Spruce	Utah	74'	Lyndon B. Johnson
As president, Johnson lit the National Community Christmas Tree in Washington, D.C. Another was lighted in the village of Hooper Bay on the Bering Sea Coast. It was the first community to be electrified by the Alaskan Village Electric Cooperative which later brought power to other isolated villages in the state.				
1969	Norway Spruce	New York	65'	Richard Nixon
Before the arrival of the president at the ceremony location, nine people were arrested on charges of disorderly conduct. They were there to protest the United States' involvement in the war in Vietnam. Other demonstrators shouted their displeasure over the situation during President Nixon's Christmas address.				
1970	White Spruce	South Dakota	78'	Richard Nixon
This was perhaps the toughest of all of the National Christmas Trees. During its journey from the Black Hills of South Dakota to Washington, D.C., the train carrying the massive timber derailed . . . not once, but twice as it traveled through Nebraska! It finally arrived in the nation's capital but on the weekend before the ceremony, it fell due to strong winds and required repairs to some of the branches. A few days following the event, a number of the lights exploded due to the fireproofing compound used on the electrical sockets. Other than that, everything went smoothly.				
1971	Douglas Fir	North Carolina	65'	Richard Nixon
A special tree recognizing the prisoners of war and soldiers who were missing in action in Southeast Asia was placed in front of the National Christmas Tree.				
1972	Engelmann Spruce	Wyoming	70'	Richard Nixon
This was the final year that a tree that had been cut down was used. In the future, only living timbers were displayed as the National Christmas Tree.				
1973– 1976	Blue Spruce	Colorado	42'	Richard Nixon (1973); Gerald Ford (1974–1976)
When Gerald Ford lit the National Christmas Tree for the first time in 1974, it brought back some fond memories. In the summer of 1936, he worked as a seasonal ranger at Yellowstone National Park, a place that is known for its wonderful trees. He spoke about those days during his speech.				

YEAR	TYPE OF TREE	HOME STATE	HEIGHT	PRESIDENT
1977	Blue Spruce	Maryland	34'	Jimmy Carter
Due to concerns about using too much energy to light the tree, some changes were made under President Carter in 1977. It was lit by 2,000 new energy-saving bulbs with a five-watt design. They were shut off each evening at midnight rather than at dawn. Under the new plan, energy usage was reduced by 74%. Today, many citizens use LED (light-emitting diodes) lights for Christmas and in their homes year-round. They last longer and require less electricity than the old standard bulbs.				
1978–2010	Blue Spruce	New York	30'	Jimmy Carter (1978–1980); Ronald Reagan (1981–1988); George H.W. Bush (1989–1992); Bill Clinton (1993–2000); George W. Bush (2001–2008); Barack Obama (2009–2010)
This sturdy timber served as the National Christmas Tree for more years (32) than any other. It also had more presidents (6) turn on its lights.				
2011–2012	Blue Spruce	New Jersey	28'5"	Barack Obama
This tree replaced the previous one that was destroyed by high winds in February 2011.				
2013–2015	Blue Spruce	Virginia	31'	Barack Obama
This tree replaced the previous one that died of complications from "transplant shock."				
2016	Balsam-Veitch Fir	Wisconsin	19'	Barack Obama
The first-ever White House Christmas Tree that came from the Badger State.				

* Denotes two trees used during these years.

Chapter 44

Valley Forge and the Christmas of 1777

When troops are called to go to war, they don't let something like the weather stop them. However, that wasn't always the case.

Many decades ago, little fighting took place during the winters of the American Revolution. That's because back in the 1700s, armies didn't have the type of equipment for their soldiers to take on the enemy in a snow storm. Because of that, they usually settled in one location for the winter and waited to begin fighting again in the spring.

For the troops under the command of General George Washington, the winter of 1777–1778 was a real life nightmare. On December 19, 1777, almost 12,000 soldiers of the Continental Army began to set up their winter camp at Valley Forge, Pennsylvania, just 18 miles from Philadelphia. They were cold, hungry, some were sick and there was already six inches of snow on the ground.

In other areas, their enemy, the British Redcoats, were warm inside comfortable quarters with plenty of food and goods for the winter.

General Washington was furious for the supplies that had not been provided and wrote a ten page letter to Congress to inform them of his feelings. Some of the American troops had become so angry that they considered a mutiny where they would overthrow Washington and take over the army themselves. They were living in crude huts which they had built that had no heat.

While British soldiers enjoyed a holiday feast, Christmas Eve dinner for Washington's soldiers consisted of a small amount of rice and vinegar. However, as bad as things were, the following day the men got together to sing songs of celebration on Christmas. As time passed, something

George Washington leading the Continental Army to Valley Forge in 1777 (painting by William B. T. Trego).

unexpected took place; instead of giving up hope, the Americans became more determined to win.

Over the following weeks, they began to forage and hunt for food. This helped them to prepare for a time when they would once again face the enemy. Even though conditions were still difficult, most of the army survived to spring when they continued the fight for independence. Their effort paid off as three years later, the British surrendered.

DID ANYTHING ELSE IN AMERICAN HISTORY HAPPEN ON CHRISTMAS?

December 25th is the recognized date for the birth of Jesus Christ which led to the day that we know as Christmas. Following that historic event, a few others followed on or near that same day during these years:

1621—Governor William Bradford of Plymouth Colony (now part of Massachusetts) forbid the playing of games on Christmas. He believed that it should be a workday like all others.

1651—The Massachusetts Bay Colony legislature officially banned Christmas and fined anyone caught celebrating a total of five shillings. They stated that to celebrate was a "great dishonor of God."

1760—Jupiter Hammon, an African American slave, composed the poetry broadside, "An Evening Thought." The following year, it became the first poem to be published that had been written by an African American.

1776—The first American Christmas tree can be credited to a Hessian soldier by the name of Henrick Roddmore, who was captured in 1776 during the Revolutionary War's Battle of Bennington. He then went to

The 1960 National Christmas Tree on its way from Oregon to Washington, D.C., by rail (photo by Abbie Rowe).

work on the farm of Samuel Denslow in Windsor Locks, Connecticut, where for the next fourteen years he put up and decorated Christmas trees in the Denslow family home.

1780—The city of Nashville, Tennessee, was founded on Christmas Day. Today, it is the state's capital.

1821—Clara Barton, an American nurse and humanitarian, founded the American Red Cross.

1842—Charles Minnegrode, an Episcopalian minister from Williamsburg introduced the custom of decorating trees in the state of Virginia.

1893—Henry Ford was curious about the new creation known as the gasoline engine. On Christmas Eve, from his rented home in Detroit, he ran an experiment as his wife Clara dripped fuel into a little motor. It ran for less than a minute but provided Ford with the knowledge of what was possible.

After that, Henry Ford went on to create one of the biggest car companies in history.

1894—In a college football game played at Palo Alto, California, on Christmas Day, the University of Chicago defeated Stanford 24–4. It made Chicago the first midwestern football team to play a game on the west coast.

However, the most famous person on the field that day was not a player. It was the team manager for Stanford who, years later, was elected president of the United States—Herbert Hoover.

1896—The patriotic song, "Stars & Stripes Forever," was written by John Philip Sousa while traveling home from Europe onboard an ocean liner. While it may have been composed on Christmas, it is usually among the songs played on the fourth of July.

In 1944, General George S. Patton lead his troops to victory on Christmas (U.S. Department of Defense photo).

1907—Oklahoma became the last state to declare Christmas a legal holiday.

1939—Robert L. May, a copywriter for the Montgomery Ward Company, created a poem about a ninth reindeer named Rudolph. He had a shiny red nose and became a hero one foggy Christmas Eve. A copy of the poem was given away to each Montgomery Ward customer.

1944—One of the most heroic acts of World War II took place on Christmas 1944. The U.S. Third Army under the command of General George Patton marched 100 miles in just forty-eight hours while it was snowing.

They crossed France advancing into the town of Bastogne (pronounced Bass-stone) in the country of Belgium.

When they arrived, they were able to free a unit of American soldiers that had been trapped by the enemy. Known as the Battle of Bastogne, it was an important victory and made for a Merry Christmas for General Patton's troops and those that they freed.

1990—The Internet was first tested on Christmas Day. The successful tryout of the earth's first server was successful using the web address info.cern.ch. It did not take place in the United States but in Geneva, Switzerland.

2004—A space probe was released from the Cassini spacecraft. It eventually landed on Saturn's moon Titan on January 14, 2005.

2006—One of the rare 1963 Christmas cards that were signed by John and Jacqueline Kennedy sold at auction for $45,000.

2013—U.S. astronauts Rick Mastracchio and Michael Hopkins took a Christmas Eve spacewalk in order to make repairs to the cooling systems of the International Space Station. The task took six-and-a-half hours.

Former presidents Harry Truman (1972) and Gerald Ford (2006) each died the day after Christmas.

William Henry Harrison.

Epilogue
William Henry Harrison and James Garfield
The 9th and 20th Presidents

No White House Christmas

There were two men who never got to celebrate Christmas while they were president. That was William Henry Harrison and James Garfield who both died during their first year in office before the holiday.

President Harrison took the oath in March 1841. He caught a cold that continued to worsen causing him problems with his breathing. The nation's new leader died after only one month as president. It is the shortest term in the nation's history.

However, in 1888, his grandson Benjamin was elected as the nation's twenty-third president and served his entire four years in office. You can read about his Christmas days in chapter 21.

In September 1881, President Garfield passed away after serving just seven months in office. He had been shot by an angry individual a few weeks earlier in the Washington, D.C., train station. After the funeral, his wife and children returned to their farm in northern Ohio.

President Garfield had four sons and one daughter. All of the boys graduated from Williams College in Massachusetts just like their father.

It's a Fact—Extra!

- John F. Kennedy and Donald Trump never met but they enjoyed traveling to the same place for Christmas. They spent the holidays in Palm Beach, Florida, where each family owned a mansion.
- During Christmastime 1795, there were rumors that George Washington would retire rather than run for another term. A few days later, he confirmed the story by informing the cabinet of his decision. However, one person who wasn't told was his vice president John Adams. Perhaps Washington didn't want him as the second president? It didn't matter, the father of the country went home to Virginia and Adams was elected the next year.
- In 1887, while Grover Cleveland was president, Peoria, Illinois, hosted the first Santa Claus Parade. The town continues this tradition today making it the longest running event of its kind in the United States In 1958, the parade began being televised.
- In 1919, President Woodrow Wilson suffered a stroke. Because of that, his wife Edith took over the running of the White House. Due to the situation, there was no Christmas tree that year and the president spent a quiet day watching a movie.
- In 1924, a new carol, "Christmas Bells" was composed by Jason Noble Pierce, the pastor at the First Congregational Church in D.C., and dedicated it to First Lady Grace Coolidge.
- An Atlas rocket was launched on December 18, 1958, and provided a first test of a communications relay system in space. The system broadcasted a Christmas message by way of shortwave radio from U.S. president Dwight D. Eisenhower through an onboard tape recorder.
- On Christmas Day, 1963, a group of family and members of the press were at Lyndon Johnson's ranch in Texas. The president's relatives were there for dinner while the media had arrived to cover the family's Christmas. Johnson was proud of his many acres and decided to take the press corps on an extensive tour. That caused Christmas dinner to be served very late, which didn't sit well with the First Lady who stated that her gravy "was not getting better with age."
- Many citizens living in New York and Vermont in 1969 surely remember Richard Nixon's first Christmas as president as a foot of snow fell on December 22. That was followed by another two feet that fell during the three-day storm. The town of Waitsfield, Vermont, topped the area with forty-four inches of snow.
- The biggest selling item for Christmas 1996, while Bill Clinton was president, was Tickle Me Elmo. It was stuffed toy version of the Muppet character from *Sesame Street* and sold in stores for $28.99.

But demand increased as Christmas drew near which had some customers paying as much as $2,000 for the little toy!, By the end of the holiday season, the entire stock of one million Tickle Me Elmo toys was sold out.
- The motion picture *The Polar Express* opened in theaters during the Christmas season of 2004 while George W. Bush was president. It was a worldwide hit and continues to be shown on television each year during the holidays.
- On December 14–15, 2008, President George W. Bush visited U.S. troops serving in Iraq and Afghanistan.
- In his eight years as president, Barack Obama went to the same place for each of them during Christmas. He traveled to his home state of Hawaii where he would reunite with friends and relatives, swim in the ocean, and play golf.

CHRISTMAS QUOTES FROM THE PRESIDENTS

"Christmas is not a time or a season but a state of mind. To cherish peace and good will, to be plenteous in mercy, is to have the real spirit of Christmas. If we think on these things, there will be born in us a Savior and over us will shine a star sending its gleam of hope to the world."
—Calvin Coolidge, 1927

"The Christmas spirit lives tonight in the bitter cold of the front lines in Europe and in the heat of the jungles and swamps of Burma and the Pacific islands. Even the roar of our bombers and fighters in the air and the guns of our ships at sea will not drown out the messages of Christmas which come to the hearts of our fighting men."
—Franklin D Roosevelt, 1944

"It is the day when we remind ourselves that man can and must live in peace with his neighbors and that it is the peacemakers who are truly blessed."
—John F. Kennedy, 1962

"On Christmas, we celebrate the birth of Christ with prayer, feasting, and great merriment. But, most of all, we experience it in our hearts. For, more than just a day, Christmas is a state of mind. It is found throughout the year whenever faith overcomes doubt, hope conquers despair, and love triumphs over hate."
—Ronald Reagan, 1981

"At Christmas, we celebrate the promise of salvation that God gave to mankind almost 2,000 years ago. The birth of Christ changed the course of history, and His life changed the soul of man. Christ taught that giving is the greatest of all aspirations and that the redemptive power of love and sacrifice is stronger than any force of arms."
—George H.W. Bush, 1991

Answer Key for Today's Questions

1—George Washington
 1. George Washington
 2. The Delaware
 3. New Jersey

2—John Adams
 1. Firewood
 2. The Adams's granddaughter
 3. It wasn't built until the last year of his one term.

3—Thomas Jefferson
 1. Dinosaur bones
 2. The violin or fiddle
 3. President Jefferson's grandson James Madison Randolph became the first child to be born at the White House.

4—James Madison
 1. Thomas Jefferson
 2. Loo
 3. It had been damaged by the British troops during the War of 1812.

5—James Monroe
 1. He stuck his finger inside the bullet hole.
 2. It was the first wedding ever held at the White House.
 3. It was painted white to cover the burn marks left by the fires started by the enemy troops during the War of 1812.

6—John Quincy Adams
 1. A green plant with leaves that are red, white, or pink
 2. They used the blooms to make red dye and medicine.
 3. Mexico

7—Andrew Jackson
 1. Christmas gifts
 2. President Jackson's bedroom
 3. The White House

8—Martin Van Buren
 1. Holland
 2. Boar's head
 3. Blue

Answer Key for Today's Questions

9—John Tyler
1. New York
2. George Washington
3. New York City

10—James K. Polk
1. Doctors and nurses at hospitals; police officers; and members of the military.
2. Mexico
3. President Polk's mother and father

11—Zachary Tyler
1. Forty years
2. Betty was the official hostess.
3. Old-fashioned coconut cakes

12—Millard Fillmore
1. Buffalo, New York
2. She quit her job as a teacher to become the official White House hostess.
3. Library of Congress

13—Franklin Pierce
1. The Pilgrims
2. The Germans
3. Outside of the White House

14—James Buchanan
1. States that left the Union
2. The Union would not allow slavery.
3. President James Buchanan

15—Abraham Lincoln
1. The Civil War
2. To help pay for the Christmas dinners for the wounded soldiers
3. Small tree branches

16—Andrew Johnson
1. Andrew Johnson
2. False
3. Christmas

17—Ulysses S. Grant
1. His gold pocket watch
2. A Christmas card
3. Hawaii

18—Rutherford B. Hayes
1. She was the first First Lady to graduate from college.
2. A handmade dollhouse
3. A $5.00 gold piece

19—Chester Arthur
1. He had it remodeled.
2. A hospital for old and disabled veterans
3. She served hot food and helped with a toy drive for poor children.

20—Grover Cleveland
1. He didn't have a family, a vice president, or a Christmas tree.
2. The White House
3. Electric lights

21—Benjamin Harrison
1. A Christmas tree
2. A crate of extra-large potatoes
3. Santa Claus

22—William McKinley
1. New York City
2. Their daughter Katie
3. A small Christmas tree

Answer Key for Today's Questions 167

23—Theodore Roosevelt
  1. He feared that forests would be destroyed because of the loss of pine trees.
  2. They hid it in a White House closet.
  3. The White House electrician

24—William Howard Taft
  1. A gift of apple pies, jellies, and jams made from fruit grown on the Torrey property
  2. The Secret Service
  3. The Blue Room

25—Woodrow Wilson
  1. Forty feet
  2. American soldiers were fighting in World War I
  3. By ship

26—Warren Harding
  1. Candles
  2. A giant-sized candy cane
  3. A radio

27—Calvin Coolidge
  1. Vermont
  2. Red, white, and green
  3. President Coolidge

28—Herbert Hoover
  1. The main building of the White House
  2. The West Wing
  3. The gate was locked and the fire department didn't have a key.

29—Franklin D. Roosevelt
  1. Christmas trees
  2. "The Night before Christmas"
  3. Out of respect for U.S. soldiers who were fighting in World War II

30—Harry S. Truman
  1. It needed to be repaired.
  2. Across the street from the White House
  3. At their home in Independence, Missouri

31—Dwight D. Eisenhower
  1. He served in the military.
  2. Golf
  3. A satellite

32—John F. Kennedy
  1. The *Nutcracker*
  2. She was mobbed by her fans.
  3. Christmas cards

33—Lyndon B. Johnson
  1. Texas
  2. "Jingle Bells"
  3. Both were serving in the military during the war in Vietnam.

34—Richard Nixon
  1. Gingerbread
  2. She wanted to share the White House decorations with as many people as possible.
  3. "Rudolph the Red-Nosed Reindeer"

35—Gerald Ford
  1. Football
  2. Colorado
  3. Two hundred years

36—Jimmy Carter
  1. Georgia
  2. Peanuts
  3. Fireworks

37—Ronald Reagan
  1. Illinois
  2. He lost his job.
  3. So that the Secret Service agents could spend the holidays with their families

38—George H.W. Bush
  1. Navy
  2. Cherry Picker
  3. Kuwait

39—Bill Clinton
  1. The president lit the city's Christmas tree.
  2. The Special Olympics
  3. A gingerbread house called the "House of Socks"

40—George W. Bush
  1. John and John Quincy Adams
  2. Red, white, and blue
  3. True

41—Barack Obama
  1. Chicago
  2. Safety
  3. President Obama

42—Donald Trump
  1. He was one of the top builders of expensive hotels and golf courses throughout the world.
  2. Central Park in New York City
  3. He loaned his family his private jet.

References

ARTICLES CONSULTED

Anderson, Bob and Karen Shahan: "Christmas Plants Brighten the Holiday Season" (Kentucky Cooperative Extension Service; June 2003)

Anthony, Carl: "First Ladies at Christmas: Six Southern Hostesses, Part 1" (National First Ladies Library; 2014)

———: "The First Ladies at Christmas: Five Victorian Ladies, Part 2" (National First Ladies Library; December 15, 2014)

———: "Christmas at the White House: First Families & Holiday Charities, Part 3" (carlanthonyonline.com; December 8, 2012)

Arce, Mark and Andrew Kaczynski: "Donald Trump Once Saved a Woman's Farm from Foreclosure" (buzzfeed.com; August 21, 2015)

Archbold, Matthew: "The President Who Banned Christmas Trees and the Boy Who Snuck One In" (*National Catholic Register*; December 3, 2014)

Barthold, Elizabeth: "Historic American Buildings Survey, Carter Peanut Warehouse Complex" (National Park Service; Summer 1989)

Barton, David: "Christmas with the Presidents" (wallbuilders.com; December 2008)

———: "Christmas—As Celebrated By the Presidents" (wallbuilders.com; December 2010)

Binker, Mary Jo: "Eleanor Roosevelt's 'My Day': Christmas" (whitehousehistory.org; November 26, 2016)

Black, Lisa: "Toy Creator Unwraps Story of Success" (*Chicago Tribune*; December 10, 1996)

Boasberg, Leonard W.: "A Letter from Washington Recalls the Cold, Hungry Christmas of 1777" (*Philadelphia Inquirer*; December 25, 1991)

Brooks, Rebecca Beatrice: "When Christmas Was Banned in Boston" (History of Massachusetts; December 5, 2011)
Brown, Floyd and Mary Beth: "Ronald Reagan's Favorite Christmas Gift" (FrontPageMagazine.com; December 24, 2008)
Bryan Jr., Charles F.: "No War on Toys: The Man Who Saved Christmas" (*Richmond Times-Dispatch*; December 1, 2013)
Bushong, William: "The Life and Presidency of Grover Cleveland" (whitehousehistory.org; retrieved December 24, 2015)
———: "The Life and Presidency of Theodore Roosevelt" (The White House Historical Association; retrieved December 29, 2015)
———: "The Life and Presidency of William Howard Taft" (White House Historical Association; retrieved January 3, 2016)
Carlson, Grant: "Christmas at the White House" (Theodore Roosevelt Center; December 21, 2011)
Clinton, Hillary Rodham: "Talking It Over" (creators.com; December 1, 1997)
Craig, Barbara: "1st Christmas Card Sent to White House" (*Reading Eagle*; December 14, 1979)
Danneberger, Karl: "Poinsettia: A Holiday Tradition" (*Buckeye Turf*; retrieved May 11, 2015)
DiBacco, Thomas V.: "'No Christmas Tree in the White House'" (*Wall Street Journal*; December 9, 2015)
Edwards, Owen: "The Day Two Astronauts Said They Saw a UFO Wearing a Red Suit" (*Smithsonian Magazine*; December 2005)
Federer, William: "215 Years Ago, the Library of Congress Began" (*Western Journalism*; April 24, 2015)
Gibbs, C. R.: "The Way We Were: How Washington Celebrated Christmas 100 Years Ago Recalling Christmas of 1886" (*Washington Post*; December 25, 1986)
Granstra, Pat: "Cristmas 1862" (*Civil War Primer*; retrieved December 17, 2015)
Grier, Peter: "A Christmas Tree Farmer as President? How He Raised Spirits during Wartime" (*Christian Science Monitor*; December 24, 2011)
Gowdy, J. D.: "The First Whitehouse Christmas with John & Abigail Adams" (The Washington, Jefferson, and Madison Institute; December 10, 2013)
Hanthaler, Joe: "5 facts about James Buchanan" (lancasteronline.com; Febuary 17, 2014)
Harrison, Eric: "Zachary Taylor Did Not Die of Arsenic Poisoning, Tests Indicate" (*Los Angeles Times*; June 27, 1991)
Heinl, Jr., Robert D.: "'Twas the Night before Christmas . . ." (firehouse.com; December 22, 2005)
Hemmer, Nicole: Day 10: "If We Just Had Our Two Boys Back and the Other 555,000 Out There" (millercenter.org; December 10, 2015)
Im, Jimmy: "Where Hillary Clinton, Donald Trump and Other Presidential Candidates Vacation" (hollywoodreporter.com; April 28, 2016)
James, Emily: "Have Yourself a Presidential Christmas!" (*UK Daily Mail*; December 4, 2015)
Janos, Leo: "The Last Days of the President" (*The Atlantic*; July 1973)
Johnson, Charles C.: "Christmas at the Coolidges" (*National Review*; December 23, 2011)

Johnson, Pamela: "Loveland Woman Decorates White House Christmas Tree" (*Loveland Reporter Herald*; December 24, 2014)

Keillor, Garrison: "The Writer's Almanac" (American Public Media; December 24, 2013)

Kelly, Kate: "The Pets in the Benjamin Harrison White House" (americacomesalive.com; August 25, 2013)

———: The White House and Holidays Past (America Comes Alive; December 27, 2013)

King, Gilbert: "The History of the Teddy Bear: From Wet and Angry to Soft and Cuddly" (Smithsonian.com; December 21, 2012)

Kovalchik, Kara: "18 Facts about Your Favorite Christmas TV Specials" (Mental Floss; December 17, 2015)

Lewis, Jamie: "President Bans Christmas Tree from White House!" (Forest History Society; December 19, 2008)

Longacre, Glenn V.: "The Christmas Tree Ship: Captain Herman E. Schuenemann and the Schooner *Rouse Simmons*" (National Archives; Winter 2006, Vol. 38, No. 4)

Lyman, Rick: "Faster and Cheaper, Trump Finishes N.Y.C. Ice Rink" (*Philadelphia Inquirer*; November 1, 1986)

Mahoney-Christopher: "First Indoor Baseball Game" (famousdaily.com; retrieved December 24, 2015)

Mast, Erin Carlson: "President Arthur's Holiday at the Soldiers' Home" (lincolnscottage.com; October 26, 2007)

McFeatters, Ann: "10 U.S. Presidents Had Irish Ancestors" (Post-Gazette.com; March 17, 2000)

McLaurin, Stewart D.: "White House Gingerbread: Holiday Traditions" (White House Historical Association; December 13, 2015)

Meyer, Theodoric and Tarini Parti: "Trump Lifts the Veil on His Empire" (politico.com; July 22, 2015)

Nolte, Carl: "S.F.'s Fiery Christmas Eve—In 1849/Gold-Rush-era Disaster Was 150 Years Ago Today" (*San Francisco Chronicle*; December 24, 1999)

Oloffson, Kristi: "From Tickle Me Elmo to Squinkies: Top 10 Toy Crazes" (*Time Magazine*; December 23, 2010)

Paramaguru, Kharunya: "NASA Astronauts Make Rare Christmas Eve Spacewalk" (time.com; December 24, 2013)

Pestano, Andrew V.: "Michelle Obama Welcomes Military Families to View Holiday Decorations" (upi.com; November 29, 2016)

Pettus, Louise: "Andrew Jackson's Christmas" (Welcome to the Waxhaws; retrieved May 13, 2015)

Putnam, John: "The First Great Fire of San Francisco" (Examiner.com; retrieved December 12, 2015)

Rankin, Robert A.: "In Bosnia, Clinton Gives Thanks to GIs Without Them, The Fighting Would Have Continued, He Said. Some Say They Aren't Convinced of Their Mission" (*Philadelphia Inquirer*; December 23, 1997)

Rawlings, Nate: "Lyndon Johnson, LBJ Ranch, Texas" (*Time Magazine*; August 18, 2011)

Righthand, Jess: "A Smithsonian Holiday Story: Joel Poinsett and the Poinsettia" (Smithsonian.com: December 6, 2010)

Rogowski, Reinhard: "President's Message" (*Medina Bugle*; Winter 2012)

Roosevelt, Theodore: "Nobel Lecture: International Peace" (Nobel Lecture; May 5, 1910)

Ross, Sonya: "Holiday Treasures at the White House" (Associated Press; December 7, 1999)

Rothman, Lily: "FDR Moved Thanksgiving to Give People More Time to Shop" (*Time Magazine*; November 28, 2014)

Secrest, William B.: *California Disasters, 1812–1899: Firsthand Accounts of Fires, Shipwrecks, Floods, Epidemics, Earthquakes and other California Tragedies* (Quill Driver Books/Word Dancer Press, Inc.; 2006)

Semmons, Ryan P. and David S. Nolen: "War and Remembrance: Walter Place and Ulysses S. Grant" (*The Primary Source*; Vol. 32, no. 2; 2013)

Sferrazza, Carl A.: "The First Families: Hosts of Christmas Past" (*Washington Post*; December 25, 1985)

Slack, Megan: "White House Holiday Decoration Preview with the First Lady" (whitehouse.gov; November 30, 2011)

Shepherd, Shawna: "Michelle Obama Previews White House's Holiday Look" (cnn.com; December 3, 2009)

Smith, Radell: "Donald Trump Good Deed Remembered, and Good Press from WSJ" (examiner.com; January 23, 2012)

Sobieraj, Sandra: "National Christmas Tree Lights Up Washington" (Associated Press; December 10, 1988)

Staff Report: "Christmas at the White House" (*Abilene Kansas Weekly Reflector*; January 3, 1884)

———: "The President's Christmas" (*New York Times*; December 28, 1884)

———: "Christmas at the White House" (*The Lutheran Witness*; January 7, 1892)

———: "The President's Christmas" (*New York Times*; December 26, 1898)

———: "Patrol of Havana" (*Cincinnati Commercial Tribune*; December 26, 1898)

———: "Christmas at White House" (*Sacramento Daily Union*; December 22, 1899)

———: "Christmas as Celebrated at the President's Home" (Hutchinson, Kansas, News, December 25, 1900)

———: "White House Frolic" (*Urbana [IL] Daily Courier*; February 11, 1904)

———: "Mr. and Mrs. Taft Lost in Capital" (*Chicago Tribune*; December 25, 1911)

———: "Taft Gives Turkeys" (American Press Association; December 28, 1911)

———: "Theodore Roosevelt Dies Suddenly at Oyster Bay Home" (*New York Times*; January 6, 1919)

———: "Good Housekeeping's Book of Menus, Recipes and Household Discoveries" (*Good Housekeeping Magazine*; third edition, 1922)

———: "White House Carols and Brilliant Tree Usher Christmas" (*Washington Post*; December 25, 1923)

———: "Amy to Get Chainsaw" (United Press International; December 7, 1977)

———: "Hallmark Produces White House Christmas Card" (United Press International; Dec. 7, 1992)

———: "Clinton Shops Online for the First Time" (CNN; December 20, 1999)

———: "Washington Crosses the Delaware, 1776" (EyeWitness to History; 2004)

_____: "Gerald R. Ford: Park Ranger, 38th President of the United States" (National Park Service; December 27, 2006)
_____: "Washington Crosses the Delaware" (history.com; 2009)
_____: "Christmas at the White House No Small Feat" (Associated Press; December 10, 2009)
_____: "White House Christmas Past" (Vintage Allies; December 3, 2010)
_____: "Hundreds of Christmas Flights Canceled as Storm Threatens East Coast" (CNN; December 25, 2010)
_____: "History of Christmas Trees" (history.com; retrieved December 15, 2012)
_____: "A White House Christmas Gallery: The Clinton Years" (*Rocky Coast News*; December 19, 2012)
_____: "Eisenhower Xmas Greeting First Space to Earth Message" (spacecoastdaily.com; December 23, 2013)
_____: "Lessons from Lincoln's last Christmas" (*Wisconsin State Journal*; December 21, 2014)
_____: "National Christmas Trees through the Years" (National Park Service; retrieved January 5, 2015)
_____: "Downstairs at the White House: State Dining Room" (The Lehrman Institute; retrieved December 16, 2015)
_____: "American History: The First Real Two-Party U.S. Presidential Election in 1796" (historynet.com; December 16, 2015)
_____: "Jackie Kennedy Has a White House Christmas or Two" (New England Historical Society; retrieved January 22, 2016)
_____: "St. Nicholas Biography" (Biography.com; retrieved January 30, 2016)
_____: "The 10 Worst Snowstorms in Northeast US in Last 60 Years" (Fox News; January 26, 2015
Swanson, James L.: "The JFK Christmas Card That Was Never Sent" (smithsonianmag.com; January 2014)
Theissen, Del Wolf: *Patton Claimed His Success in Battle Was Divinely Willed* (Agave Publishers LLC; March 22, 2014)
Tilt, Ken and Bernice Fischman: "History of the Christmas Tree" (auburn.edu; received December 14, 2015)
Troy, Gil: "The Worst White House Christmases Ever" (dailybeast.com; December 25, 2015)
Waldroup, Regina: "Chicago Boy's Letter to Santa Asking for Safety Gets Reply from Obama" (nbcchicago.com; December 29, 2014)
Weintraub, Boris: "All Traditions of the Yule Season Mark White House Celebrations" (National Geographic News Service; December 18, 1986)
Williams, Marjorie: "Barbara's Backlash" (*Vanity Fair Magazine*; January 1, 2007)
Williams, Richard G. Jr.: "America's First Christmas tree" (*Washington Times*; December 8, 2006)
Wullenjohn, Chuck C.: "Christmas Comes to a Post-War World—70 Year Anniversary of the End of World War II" (army.mil; December 9, 2015)

BOOKS CONSULTED

Allen, William C.: *History of the United States Capitol: A Chronicle of Design, Construction, and Politics* (Government Printing Office; 2001)

Byrnes, Mark Eaton: *James K. Polk: A Biographical Companion* (ABC-CLIO; 2001)
Carter, Jimmy: *Christmas in Plains: Memories* (Simon & Schuster; 2001)
Cole, Donald B.: *Martin van Buren and the American Political System* (Princeton University Press; 2014)
Crump, William D.: *The Christmas Encyclopedia, 3rd edition* (McFarland; 2013)
Daniel, Margaret Truman: *Harry S. Truman* (William Morrow & Co.; 1972)
Gould, Lewis L.: *The William Howard Taft Presidency* (University Press of Kansas; 2009)
———: *American First Ladies: Their Lives and Their Legacy* (Routledge; 2014)
Gulevich, Tanya: *Encyclopedia of Christmas and New Year's Celebrations, 2nd edition* (Omnigraphics, Inc.; 2003)
Havelin, Kate: *Ulysses S. Grant* (Lerner Publishing Group; 2003)
Henry, Mike: *Black History: More Than Just a Month* (Rowman & Littlefield; 2012)
Hewson, Martha S. and Walter Cronkite: *John Quincy Adams* (Chelsea House Publications; January 2004)
Jeffers, Harry Paul: *Legends of Santa Claus* (Twenty-First Century Books; 2000)
Kelly, Brian C.: *Best Little Stories from the White House: More Than 100 True Stories* (Cumberland House; 2012)
Lurie, Jonathan: *William Howard Taft: The Travails of a Progressive Conservative* (Cambridge University Press; 2014)
May, Gary: *John Tyler: The American Presidents Series: The 10th President, 1841–1845* (Henry Holt and Company; 2008)
Menendez, Albert J.: *Christmas in the White House* (Westminster John Knox Press; 1983)
Moore, Anne Chieko and Hester Anne Hale: *Benjamin Harrison: Centennial President* (Nova Science Publishing, Inc.; 2006)
Pringle, Henry F.: *The Life and Times of William Howard Taft* (American Political Biography Press; 1998)
Rasenberger, Jim: *America, 1908: The Dawn of Flight, the Race to the Pole, the Invention of the Model T, and the Making of a Modern Nation* (Scribner; 2011)
Scarry, Robert J.: *Millard Fillmore* (McFarland & Co. Inc.; 2010)
Seale, William Seale: *The President's House: A History* (White House Historical Association with the cooperation of the National Geographic Society; 1986)
Staff: *Christmas in Colonial and Early America (Christmas Around the World)* (World Book Inc.; 1997)
———: *Christmas in Washington, D. C.* (World Book; 1998)
Taylor, Jon: *Harry Truman's Independence: The Center of the World* (The History Press; 2013)
Traxel, David: *1898: The Birth of the American Century* (Alfred A. Knopf, Inc.; 1998)
Treese, Joe D. and Evan Phifer: *The Christmas Eve West Wing Fire of 1929* (whitehousehistory.org; February 9, 2016)
Walsh, Kenneth T.: *Celebrity in Chief: A History of the Presidents and the Culture of Stardom* (Paradigm Publishers; 2015)
Weeks, Philip: *Buckeye Presidents: Ohioans in the White House* (Kent State University Press; 2003)
Ziemann, Hugo: *The Original Whitehouse Cookbook—1887 Facsimilie Edition* (Devin Adair; 1983)

References

WEBSITES CONSULTED

44diaries.com
aam.govst.edu
almanac.com
blackfriday.com
bush41.org
bushcenter.org
christmasseals.org
cliffordawright.com
clintonlibrary.gov
digitalhistory.uh.edu
eisenhower.archives.gov
fdrlibrary.org
foodtimeline.org
fordlibrarymuseum.gov
freepublic.com
friendsofsoldiers.org
georgewbush-whitehouse.archives.gov
history.com
history.state.gov
hoover.archives.gov
jfklibrary.org
jimmycarterlibrary.gov
lbjlibrary.org
lincolnslunch.com
loc.gov
millercenter.org
nixonlibrary.gov
noaa.gov
nps.gov
presidentbenjaminharrison.org
presqueisle.mainememory.net
reaganfoundation.org
trumanlibraryinstitute.org
weatherdb.com
whitehouse.gov
whitehousechristmascards.com
woodrowwilson.org

IMAGES

All photo and artist renderings are listed below the work, unless they are in the public domain.

About the Author

For thirty-one years, **Mike Henry** taught American history to students at all levels of the educational spectrum from elementary school to college. His technique of using the events of the past to show how they impact our lives in the present made him a popular classroom instructor and guest speaker. After the inception of No Child Left Behind, he averaged a success rate of more than 80 percent on mandated testing where the majority of his students were at or below the poverty level.

Mike is a two-time award winner of Who's Who Among America's Classroom Teachers. Following his retirement, he wrote *Black History: More Than Just a Month*, which was published in 2012. The book has become popular among those wanting to learn more and for educators of African American history.

What They Didn't Teach You in American History Class was released in 2014 and nominated for the James Harvey Robinson Prize. Its sequel, *What They Didn't Teach You in Your American History Class: The Second Encounter* debuted in 2016. These works are for those who are interested in learning about the interesting backstories that are not included in most history texts.

In 2015, Mike introduced his *American History for Kids* series. The first volume, *Tell Me about the Presidents* was nominated for the Grateful American Book Prize. All of the author's works are published by Rowman & Littlefield.

The follow-up effort is titled Christmas with the presidents. It tells how our nation's leaders spent their holiday seasons ranging from the simple to the elaborate and even heroic.

"True education begins with reading," said the author. "Once that takes place, learning can happen with any subject matter."

Mike and his wife Pamela, who is also a retired educator and co-editor of his books, reside near Dallas, Texas.

www.ingramcontent.com/pod-product-compliance
Lightning Source LLC
Chambersburg PA
CBHW031552300426
44111CB00006BA/284